My Southern Food

My Southern Food

A Celebration of the Flavors of the South

DEVON O'DAY

EDITED BY BRYAN CURTIS

THOMAS NELSON
Since 1798

NASHVILLE   DALLAS   MEXICO CITY   RIO DE JANEIRO

Published in Nashville, Tennessee, by Thomas Nelson. Thomas Nelson is a registered trademark of Thomas Nelson, Inc.

Photos on pages xii, 3, 6, 8, 10, 12, 17, 20, 23, 24, 26, 30, 32, 35, 36, 37, 40, 42, 47, 48, 51, 53, 55, 56, 59, 62, 64,
67, 68, 73, 74, 79, 85, 86, 89, 92, 95, 97, 98, 102, 105, 106, 109, 110, 113, 114, 117, 122, 125, 126, 128, 131, 133, 135, 136, 139,
141, 145, 146, 149, 151, 152, 154, 157, 161, 162, 165, 166, 169, 171, 172, 174, 175, 176, 180, 183, 185, 187, 188, 190, 193, 194, 197, 201,
204, 207, 209, 210, 212, 214, 217, 218, 221, 222, 226, 231, 235, 236, 239, 242, and 245 licensed through Shutterstock.

Photos on pages 29, 80, 100, and 233 licensed through iStockphoto.

Photos on pages vi and 228 by Danielle Patton.

Photo on page 121 by Ron Miller.

Photos on pages v, viii, x, 27, 142, 202, 240, and 246 are from the collection of Devon O'Day.

Art direction and design by Angie Davis Jones, One Woman Show Design.

Thomas Nelson, Inc. titles may be purchased in bulk for educational, business, fund-raising,
or sales promotional use. For information, please e-mail SpecialMarkets@ThomasNelson.com.

Library of Congress Cataloging-in-Publication Data

O'Day, Devon, 1962–
     My Southern food : a celebration of the flavors of the South /
Devon O'Day ; edited by Bryan Curtis.
   p. cm.
Includes index.
ISBN 978-1-4016-0000-6
1. Cookery, American—Southern style. I. Title.
TX715.2.S68O33 2010
641.5975—dc22
              2010020853

Printed in the United States of America

10 11 12 13 14 WCT 6 5 4 3 2 1

To my mother, Patricia Walker Ford, without whom this book would never have been written. Thank you for taking the time to pass down the legacy to Faith and me.

Contents

Foreword
Faith Ford

Growing up as sisters from a long line of seasoned Southern cooks, Devon and I were taught by the best! In fact, Devon was very instrumental in encouraging me, her skinny little sister, Faith, to take the first bite of all the family favorites: chicken and dumplings, crispy brown biscuits with cane syrup, pan-fried okra, butter beans, and fresh-sliced summer tomatoes, to name a few.

My sister was my idol. Whatever she did, I tried my best to follow along. She did everything with such grace and ease. I guess you'd say I had big shoes to fill. She was the first to read, the first to play an instrument, the first to get straight A's. And, of course, the first to cook. She would make the best oven-baked cheese toast and Cheddar-stuffed broiled hot dogs with quick skillet pork and beans of any Southern sister I knew. And these were just after-school snacks. At suppertime, she would always let me have the crispy skin off her fried chicken. The golden brown edges from the fried pork chops were my favorite. She even figured out that she could take a piece of white bread, spoon my favorite purple hull peas inside, and slip it to me across the table as if it were my own special delicacy. It was all about how quickly and efficiently she prepared and presented it.

My sister has always had a knack for throwing things together on the fly, yet seeming as if she'd worked on them for hours. It's enough to make a little sister slightly intimidated, but not me. Not around Devon. She wouldn't have that. She insisted on sharing all her tips and skills, just like our mom taught her. What's good for the hen is good for the chicks!

Devon loved going to restaurants and then coming home to whip up a quick version for us. And it was always tasty and satisfying. She always made enough for a crew too. That's another thing she got from our mom—always make enough. If it doesn't get eaten, you'll have plenty of leftovers. Turkey chili for ten, or more. Pasta as a side dish only. Cornbread for a crew. Brisket for a bevy. And casseroles that can feed a church.

Yep! That's right! My sister is a pack leader when it comes to preparing delicious, simple Southern meals. And she knows how to do it on a budget. Devon is a force in the kitchen and, just like me, she's dedicated to preserving those precious recipes of our childhood years. Trust me, after you've tried them, you'll want to pass them on too.

Introduction

I was born and raised in the red-dirt crested bluffs and bayous of north and central Louisiana. My family of wonderful cooks kept the food for our holidays, church dinners on the ground, and family reunions so special that it created a magnetic pull that kept us returning no matter where life called us.

Southern food is soulful, sinful, and satisfying in a way that no other cuisine can match. It's not only the food, but also the lifestyle that goes with it, that creates an indelible mark that time and distance cannot erase. From Acadiana's spicy kick to New Orleans's ethnic influence, to Memphis' barbecue to coastal Alabama and Mississippi River catches, Southern food is a broad palate of culinary brushstrokes. It's not a rich man's cuisine, nor is it prepared only by the highly educated food aficionado. It's accessible and real, comfortable and sustaining.

This book is my tribute to the place I call home, the food we serve, and the people who have joined me around the table and shared their fellowship and recipes with me. It is my sincere hope that the custom of eating around a table with good fresh-cooked meals can return to homes everywhere and heal something that has been lost through our busy schedules, which often make us turn to convenience food eaten on the run. At the end of our days, we won't remember the calories we counted or the time we didn't spend with those we love. But we will remember the indulgence of an incredible meal, the slow-as-molasses front-porch conversations, and the smell of bacon cooked in a real kitchen, with grace being said. The haunting perfume of wisteria, heavy hug of humidity, and tempting crunch of fried chicken will fix anything broken in life, if someone you love tells you to pull up a chair.

Sweet Tea, Cornbread, and Fried Chicken

Sunday Dinner and Other Family Gatherings

Sunday dinner is the special meal of every Southern week. It follows church. That's the way it's done. You don't miss church to prepare the meal. You cook ahead, and everyone pitches in to get the meal on the table. Everyone helps clean up. Then you take a nap, a long nap. Every holiday in the South is centered around the familiar. You don't try new recipes. You make the favorites that show up every year, made by the same person and served in the same bowl. Special occasions in the South aren't for branching out into new horizons. In the South, a special-occasion meal is to remind you of who you were and where you came from. It's that simple.

In the South, there is a delicacy known as "sweet tea."

It's not sweetened tea. It's not unsweetened tea that you add sugar to at the table.

It's prepared by mixing the hot brew with the sugar until it's dissolved into a nice thick syrup, a sort of tea concentrate, and then the cold water is added and poured over ice in the glasses.

Lemon and mint are added in some of the uptown places, but only to the glasses.

Tea, sweet tea that is, is a very individual taste.

Iced tea is always the beverage of choice in the South.

Southern Sweet Tea

Lemon slices or fresh mint leaves can be used as a garnish or flavor boost for special occasions. The amount of sugar can also be adjusted from sweet to syrup-like, coma-inducing sweet. This version is somewhere in the middle.

2	cups water
3	family-size tea bags or 6 regular-size tea bags
1	cup sugar
	About 2 cups cold water
	Lemon slices or fresh mint leaves for garnish

Bring the 2 cups water to a boil in a pot. Once boiling, add the tea bags and remove from the heat. Allow the tea bags to steep until the water is a dark red-amber color. While the tea is still hot, remove the tea bags and add the sugar, stirring until dissolved. Pour the tea syrup into a serving pitcher with the 2 cups cold water and stir. When blended, top the pitcher off with cold water until it is full. Pour over ice in glasses. Garnish with the lemon slices or mint.

Makes 6 servings

Lemonade-Stand Lemonade

Lemonade is one of those great Southern-porch-on-a-hot-afternoon traditions. It was served around three in the afternoon on our porch, usually following the midday nap. It was the boost before heading back into the fields to plow cotton or soybeans.

I prefer my lemonade a bit more tart. Adjusting the sugar to lemon juice ratio is a personal preference based on experience and response from partakers.

1½   cups sugar
½   cup boiling water
2   cups freshly squeezed lemon juice, with some pulp
6   cups cold water
     Thin lemon slices for garnish
     Ice cubes
     Crushed ice

In a large bowl combine the sugar and boiling water until the sugar granules are dissolved. (This is the same procedure used for making sweet tea. Sandy granules at the bottom of a glass are yucky and just so "not Southern.") Add the lemon juice and cold water to the prettiest clear pitcher you have. Stir the hot sugar water into the lemon mixture until completely blended. Add the lemon slices to the pitcher and then the ice cubes for a pretty, frosty, refreshing presentation. Serve over the crushed ice.

Makes 4 servings

Broccoli, Bacon, and Raisin Salad

Sweet, salty, smoky, and delicious, this salad will make even broccoli haters consider a bite. I first enjoyed a similar recipe at my friend Michael's restaurant, Monell's Southern Cooking, in Nashville, Tennessee. This is my attempt at re-creation.

1	bunch broccoli, chopped into bite-size florets
½	cup finely chopped red onion
½	cup chopped celery
½	cup grated carrots
1	pound bacon, fried, drained, and crumbled
½	cup chopped walnuts
½	cup raisins
¾	cup Miracle Whip
¼	cup sugar
2	tablespoons red wine vinegar
¼	teaspoon salt
¼	teaspoon Cajun seasoning

In a large bowl combine all the ingredients. Cover and refrigerate for at least 1 hour to marinate. Serve chilled.

Makes 6 to 8 servings

The custom of family members gathered around a table, enjoying the fruits of their labors, doesn't have to be a lost custom. It doesn't have to be just a Southern custom, although it is very ingrained in our culture. The choice to join together at a meal of homemade goodness is just that, a choice. And creating a new tradition of having meals as a family happens one meal at a time.

Aunt Brenda's Make-Ahead Seven-Layer Salad

This salad is so pretty when served in a large clear bowl, so the layers can shine through. My Aunt Brenda swears by Hellmann's mayonnaise. I like Miracle Whip. It's survival of the fittest, so whoever is the head matriarch of the table usually wins.

1	pound bacon
1	large head iceberg lettuce or 2 heads crisp romaine lettuce, chopped
1	large red Bermuda onion, chopped
1	(10-ounce) package frozen green peas, thawed
1	cup chopped green bell pepper
1¼	cups mayonnaise
10	ounces Cheddar cheese, shredded

Fry or broil the bacon, drain on paper towels, crumble, and set aside. In a large clear bowl, layer the lettuce, onion, peas, bell pepper, mayonnaise, and cheese. Top with the bacon crumbles. Cover with plastic wrap and chill.

Makes 8 to 10 servings

Crunchy-Edge Black-Skillet Cornbread

I always love hot cornbread slathered with butter. My dad loved it cold, crumbled in big chunks in a tall glass of cold buttermilk. From soup, to beans, to dressing on Thanksgiving, cornbread is the staple that the South depends on most—after bacon.

2	tablespoons bacon grease, vegetable oil, or shortening
2	cups yellow cornmeal
1	cup self-rising flour
1	teaspoon baking powder
1/2	teaspoon salt
1	teaspoon sugar
1	large egg
2	cups milk

Preheat the oven to 425 degrees. Heat the bacon grease, oil, or shortening in a 9-inch cast-iron skillet on top of the stove. (The key to good cornbread is a hot skillet.) In a large bowl combine the cornmeal, flour, baking powder, salt, sugar, egg, and milk until well mixed, and then beat vigorously for about 1 minute to add air to the mixture. Pour the mixture into the hot skillet. (The batter should sizzle as it is poured into the skillet.) Bake for 30 to 35 minutes, or until golden brown.

Makes 8 to 12 servings

PBR Bread

Interestingly enough, this recipe is adapted from one I found in a church cookbook some thirty years ago. PBR stands for Pabst Blue Ribbon beer—you can experiment with other beers, but the bread won't be as Southern as one made with PBR. The beer serves as yeast, and the coarse bread is best served warm with lots of butter. It makes a great accompaniment to soups and stews.

3   **cups self-rising flour**
5   **tablespoons sugar**
⅛   **teaspoon salt**
1   **(12-ounce) can Pabst Blue Ribbon beer, at room temperature (this is important!)**
4   **tablespoons butter, melted**

Preheat the oven to 350 degrees. Grease a 9 x 5 x 3-inch loaf pan. Sift together the flour, sugar, and salt at least 3 times. Stir in the beer, making a dough/batter, and pour into the prepared pan. Bake for 40 minutes. Remove the bread from the oven and increase the oven temperature to 375 degrees. Carefully pour the melted butter across the top of the loaf, return the bread to the oven, and bake for 15 minutes.

Makes 8 servings

Mrs. Girlinghouse's Master Mix for Biscuits

My home economics teacher, Mrs. Girlinghouse, amazed me when she taught us all how to prepare this master mix. It made everything easy. She explained that sifting added air and created light fluffiness to anything baked with the master mix. We resifted after storing the mix, before making a recipe. We used it for biscuits, cookie dough, dumplings, and other recipes. I felt like she'd introduced me to the holy grail of Southern cooking!

9	cups all-purpose flour
½	cup baking powder
1	tablespoon salt
2	teaspoons cream of tartar
¼	cup sugar
2	cups butter-flavored shortening (regular shortening works, of course, but this is a taste preference)

In a large bowl sift the flour, baking powder, salt, cream of tartar, and sugar together at least 3 times. Cut in the shortening with a pastry cutter until the texture is grainy. Store in an airtight container for up to 2 months, or indefinitely in the freezer. Use for any recipes in which you would normally use Bisquick: biscuits, pancakes, waffles, dumplings, and so on.

Makes 3 quarts

Pancake/Waffle Batter

1	cup master mix (see above)
½	cup milk
1	large egg

Combine the ingredients in a large bowl.

Makes 4 to 6 pancakes or waffles

Biscuits

1	cup master mix (see above)
¼	cup milk

Preheat the oven to 450 degrees. Combine the ingredients in a large bowl. Roll out on a floured surface and cut to the desired size. Bake for 10 minutes, or until golden brown.

Makes 6 biscuits

Cathead Cheese Biscuits

These are called "cathead" because they puff up to the size of a little cat's head. They aren't rolled and cut like biscuit-cutter biscuits.

Biscuits

2	**cups master mix (page 8) or Bisquick**
½	**cup cold milk**
¾	**cup grated sharp Cheddar cheese**

Glaze

4	**tablespoons butter, melted**
½	**teaspoon salt**
½	**teaspoon garlic powder**
½	**teaspoon Italian seasoning**

To make the biscuits, preheat the oven to 450 degrees. In a large bowl combine the master mix, milk, and cheese. Drop by large spoonfuls somewhat uniform in size on a greased baking sheet. Bake for 8 to 10 minutes on a rack in the center of the oven. Remove from the oven and switch the temperature to broil.

To make the glaze, combine all the glaze ingredients in a small bowl. Brush the tops of the biscuits with the glaze. Return the biscuits to the oven and allow the tops to get crispy under the broiler. This will only take about 2 minutes. Do *not* leave the biscuits unattended, as they can easily burn. Serve hot with butter.

Makes 10 to 12 biscuits

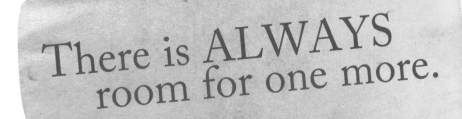

There is ALWAYS room for one more.

North Louisiana Dutch-Oven Fried Chicken

My mother taught me how to fry chicken in a big, black cast-iron skillet without a lid. That's the way my grandma did it. The grease pops out and you'd get an occasional blister when the molten fat made contact with your skin. It wasn't until I'd left home and Mom consulted with some of the cafeteria workers at South Alexandria Primary School, where she was a teacher, that she learned to use a covered Dutch oven to seal in the juices and fry tender, perfect chicken—no pops, no burns. They also told her to remember the basics: brown on the outside, reduce heat, and cook through.

1   **(2- to 3-pound) whole fryer, cut in pieces**
     Shortening or vegetable oil, to fill a cast-iron Dutch oven half full (about 3 cups)
2   **cups all-purpose flour**
2   **teaspoons salt, divided**
2   **teaspoons pepper, divided**

Rinse the chicken pieces and set aside. Heat the shortening or oil in the Dutch oven on high heat or to about 365 degrees. In a large bowl or brown paper bag, combine the flour, 1 teaspoon of the salt, and 1 teaspoon of the pepper. Use the remaining 1 teaspoon salt and remaining 1 teaspoon pepper to cover each piece of chicken before dredging in flour or shaking to coat in a brown paper bag. (Note: Additional salt and pepper, or dry Cajun seasoning, can be used on chicken pieces prior to flouring if a more savory chicken is desired.) Make sure each piece of chicken is completely covered in flour. Test the oil to make sure it is hot enough by dropping a pinch of flour in the skillet. If the flour begins to sizzle, the temperature is right. Gently add all the chicken to the Dutch oven and clamp the lid on, reducing the heat to medium-high, which should look like a gentle rolling boil. Check the chicken after about 15 minutes, bringing the bottom pieces to the top, rotating the top pieces to the bottom. At about 25 minutes remove the lid, increase the heat, and turn each piece until it becomes a dark golden brown and the juices run clear. Remove each piece with tongs or a large fork and place on a large plate covered with paper towels or brown paper to soak up any excess oil, before moving to a serving platter.

Makes 4 servings

Pat's Pot Roast

My mother is a master at roasts. She would put a roast on to cook before we left for church, and by the time we got home, the entire house was the most delicious-smelling place on earth. We'd run to change out of our church clothes and get the table set just in time for that roast to come out of the oven. The same practice was used for pork roasts and venison roasts too. The only time we'd have a problem was if the preacher got long-winded or if too many people ended up at the altar needing prayer. My dad was a deacon, and sometimes this took forever. The only thing that took precedence over a good Sunday meal in the South was Jesus.

1	(3- to 4-pound) lean chuck roast (this works with pork roast as well)
2	teaspoons seasoning salt, plus additional for sprinkling (I like Uncle Leon's for a spicy kick, but Lawry's and Tony Chachere's are also good)
1	teaspoon pepper, plus additional for sprinkling
1/4	teaspoon garlic powder
1/2	cup all-purpose flour
3	tablespoons olive oil
2	medium onions, chopped
2	stalks celery, peeled and cut in large chunks
4	cups water, divided
6	large carrots, peeled and cut in thirds
6	large potatoes, peeled and cut in large chunks
4	tablespoons butter

Preheat the oven to 350 degrees. Wash and pat dry the roast, and rub with the seasoning salt, pepper, and garlic powder. Coat the entire roast in flour. In a large roaster or Dutch oven, sear the roast over high heat in the oil until browned on all sides. Make sure any flour on the sides of the pot is scraped off and browned as you do this. Reduce the heat to medium-high and add the onions around the roast. Sauté until the onions begin to change color. Layer the celery over the roast, and pour in 3 cups of the water. Cover tightly and roast in the oven for 1 hour. Open the roaster and layer the carrots and potatoes on top. Sprinkle with additional seasoning salt and pepper, and dot with butter. Do not stir. Cover and roast for 1 more hour or until the vegetables and roast are tender. Transfer the roast to a large serving platter and spoon the vegetables around it. Or serve the vegetables in a large serving dish and the roast on a carving plate. Add the remaining 1 cup water to the meat juices and stir over medium-high heat on top of the stove until well blended to make a gravy. Scrape any browned flour from the sides and bottom to give the natural gravy plenty of body. When hot, transfer to a gravy boat and serve quickly while the meat and vegetables are still hot.

Makes 6 to 8 servings

Grillin' Chops

6	(1-inch-thick) pork chops
½	cup olive oil
2	garlic cloves, minced
1	teaspoon salt
1	teaspoon lemon pepper
4	ounces Worcestershire sauce

Wash the pork chops well, dry, and set aside. Combine the oil, garlic, salt, and lemon pepper to create a marinade. Pour over the chops in a shallow baking dish and coat the pork chops well. Cover and refrigerate for at least 1 hour. Remove the chops from the marinade and set the marinade aside. Grill the pork chops over medium coals for 25 to 30 minutes, or until no pink remains, turning several times. Add the Worcestershire sauce to the reserved marinade and baste during the last 10 minutes of cooking. (These chops are also delicious done in the oven at 350 degrees for 45 minutes until all the pink is gone, turning once and basting throughout cooking. A browning bag keeps the chops tender.)

Makes 6 servings

I go to a little white church on a hill in Kingston Springs, Tennessee. In these days of megachurches, I'm comforted that this small place of worship has been frozen in time, steeped in the color and familiarity that made me love church when I was small. With that down-home feel of a church where everybody knows everybody, there are church homecomings and dinners just like there used to be. Brenda Allen brings her smoked ham that's slow roasted and so tender it falls apart.

I swear it's the most amazing thing I've ever tasted.

Sunday-Go-to-Meetin' Chicken Pot Pie

You can chop the vegetables ahead of time and cook the chicken while the piecrust is chilling.

Make-Ahead Icebox Piecrust

1½	cups all-purpose flour
1½	teaspoons salt
5	tablespoons cold butter
¼	cup butter-flavored shortening
4½	tablespoons ice water

Pie Filling

1½	pounds boneless, skinless chicken breasts
	About 3 cups water
1	teaspoon garlic powder, divided
1	teaspoon salt, divided
1	teaspoon pepper, divided
1	medium onion, diced
2	large carrots, peeled and diced

2	tablespoons olive oil
4	tablespoons butter
½	cup all-purpose flour
1	cup cream
1	cup sliced mushrooms (drain if using canned or jarred mushrooms)
1	cup frozen green peas or whole sugar snap peas
½	teaspoon dried thyme
½	teaspoon dried basil
2	egg whites whisked with 2 tablespoons water

To make the piecrust, combine the flour and salt in a medium bowl. Cut in the butter and shortening with a pastry cutter until a coarse mealy texture. Add the ice water and mix with a fork until the dough holds together. Wrap in plastic and refrigerate overnight or at least 30 minutes before using. On a floured surface, roll out the dough to at least a 12-inch-diameter circle to cover the pie in a skillet or to a 14-inch rectangular length to cover a baking dish. Set aside.

To make the pie filling, cover the chicken in about 3 cups of water in a large pot. Add ½ teaspoon of the garlic powder, ½ teaspoon of the salt, and ½ teaspoon of the pepper. Cook the chicken until tender and cooked through. Remove the chicken from the broth and cool, reserving 1 cup chicken broth. Chop the chicken into bite-size chunks and set aside. Preheat the oven to 400 degrees. In a large skillet sauté the onion and carrots in the oil until tender. Spoon them over the chicken in a large bowl. Melt the butter in the same skillet on low heat, whisking in the flour when the butter is completely melted to form a sauce. When the sauce is smooth, gradually add the reserved 1 cup chicken broth, whisking constantly to prevent lumps. Add the cream and continue blending into a creamy sauce. Gradually stir in the mushrooms, peas, chicken mixture, thyme, basil, remaining ½ teaspoon garlic powder, remaining ½ teaspoon salt, and remaining ½ teaspoon pepper until completely blended. Cover the skillet with the round crust, or transfer the pie filling to a 13 x 9-inch baking dish and cover with the rectangular crust, cutting the excess from around the sides with a sharp knife. Bake the pie for 20 minutes. Remove from the oven and use a pastry brush to brush the crust with the egg white mixture. Return the pie to the oven and bake for 10 more minutes.

Makes 6 to 8 servings

Cider House Ham

Do not discard the ham bone when you slice this. This will yield the perfect ham hock for your black-eyed peas.

1	(5- to 6-pound) bone-in country ham
2½	cups firmly packed brown sugar, divided
1	gallon apple cider
1½	cups honey or maple syrup

The ham preparation begins with washing. If you are using a salt-cured dry ham, to rehydrate the ham, place the ham in a bowl with water to cover and soak in the refrigerator overnight (or for at least 4 hours). Pour off the water and cut off any mold or hard rind that may have formed. Pat the ham dry.

Preheat the oven to 325 degrees. Rub the outside of the ham with ¾ cup of the brown sugar and place in a large oven roaster pan with a lid. Pour in enough apple cider to cover two-thirds of the ham. Sprinkle the exposed part of the ham with ¾ cup of the brown sugar, cover, and bake for 1 hour. (Bone-in hams should bake in a traditional oven for 20 to 25 minutes per pound, with an inner temperature of 140 to 165 degrees when done.) At the end of 1 hour, pour off the cider. Add the remaining cider, cover with the remaining 1 cup brown sugar, and drizzle with the honey or syrup. Bake for 1 more hour (the cooking time is based on a 6-pound ham).

Makes 10 to 12 servings

Growing up in the South, there was always something cooking. I can't remember home and not think of the delicious smell of something *baking, broiling, roasting, simmering,* or, of course, *frying* in the kitchen.

Smokin' Bag Brisket

This same recipe can be prepared on a closed grill, without the browning bag. Brisket is wonderful as an entrée or served warm on a salad. It also makes a great po' boy, served on French bread with mayonnaise, spicy mustard, lettuce, and tomato.

1	(6- to 8-pound) lean beef brisket
2	teaspoons salt
3	tablespoons garlic powder
3	teaspoons pepper
1	large oven baking/browning bag
1	cup (4 to 5 ounces) liquid smoke, divided
1	cup (4 to 5 ounces) Worcestershire sauce, divided

Wash the brisket and rub with the salt, garlic powder, and pepper. Place the brisket in the baking bag, fat side up. Cover the meat with half the liquid smoke and half the Worcestershire sauce, and seal the bag. Place the bagged meat on a long shallow baking pan or dish, and refrigerate overnight.

Preheat the oven to 275 degrees, and place the bagged brisket on a baking pan in the oven for 5 hours. Remove from the oven, open the bag, and cover the brisket with the remaining liquid smoke and the remaining Worcestershire sauce. Close the bag and bake for 1 more hour. Carefully remove the brisket and place on a serving platter. Pour the juice from the bag into a gravy boat and serve with the brisket.

Makes 6 to 10 servings

Devon's Sausage and Rice Dressing

My family now calls this dressing a family tradition, and even takes credit for the recipe. But I actually came up with this dish for a recipe competition at a company dinner and I took home the prize. With that validation, I tried it on the real judges of my cooking, my family. It's been on our holiday table ever since, which must mean I did something right.

1	**(6-ounce) package instant wild rice mix**
1	**pound ground pork sausage with sage**
1	**onion, chopped**
1	**(10.5-ounce) can cream of mushroom soup**
1	**teaspoon Cajun seasoning**
2	**green onions, chopped**
½	**cup sliced mushrooms, drained if canned or jarred**
2	**cups shredded Cheddar cheese**

Preheat the oven to 325 degrees. Prepare the wild rice according to the package directions. In a separate skillet, brown the sausage like ground meat and sauté with the onion. In a large bowl, blend the rice, the sausage mixture, soup, Cajun seasoning, green onions, and mushrooms. Pour into a 13 x 9-inch baking dish. Top with the cheese and bake for 20 to 25 minutes, or until bubbly.

Makes 6 to 8 servings

Fresh Yellow Squash and Caramelized Onions

3	tablespoons bacon grease
6	large yellow squash, washed and sliced into medallions
½	large sweet onion, sliced
1	tablespoon sugar
1	tablespoon salt
½	teaspoon pepper

In a large cast-iron skillet, heat the bacon grease. Add the squash and onion, and sprinkle the sugar and salt evenly through the vegetables as they sauté. The sugar will begin to caramelize the onion, and the squash will begin to get tender. Cook until the vegetables are tender and the onion is golden brown, 15 to 20 minutes. Stir in the pepper just before serving.

Makes 6 to 8 servings

The colors of the Southern Sunday dinner table were always so pretty to me.

The golden color of fried chicken next to a gravy boat of dark brown gravy; a plate of bright red tomatoes, sliced, chilled, and plated with mint green cucumbers and a multihued salad; a yellow squash skillet; and a bowl of light green baby limas—these colors just begin to describe the required palate for any of our meals. I was taught early to always have lots of color on the table, and that didn't refer to the dishes and the linens.

Gas-Free Black-Eyed Peas with Christmas Ham Hock

Black-eyed peas are a traditional Southern good-luck/good-health dish on New Year's Day. Often a dime is cooked in the peas for financial good fortune. The person who ends up finding the dime in his or her New Year black-eyed peas is the one who'll be granted the most luck in the coming year. Of course, you won't feel so lucky if you swallow the dime, so be careful!

1	(16- to 20-ounce) package dried black-eyed peas
1	medium onion, chopped
1	slice bacon, quartered
	Ham hock
1	large bell pepper, chopped
1	teaspoon salt
1	teaspoon pepper
1	teaspoon Cajun seasoning
1	packet dried pea seasoning, to taste (the packet that comes in the bag of peas)
	About 4 cups water

Wash and soak the black-eyed peas overnight (8 to 12 hours) in a covered saucepan in the refrigerator. Prior to cooking, drain and wash the peas. Set aside. In a large cooking pot, sauté the onion with the bacon. Add the ham hock, peas, bell pepper, salt, pepper, Cajun seasoning, dried pea seasoning to taste, and enough water to cover the peas by about 2 inches. Bring to a rolling boil over high heat. Reduce the heat, cover, and simmer for 1½ to 2 hours, or until the peas are tender. You are hoping for a "brothy" gravy, not a paste.

Makes 6 to 8 servings

New Year's Day Good-Luck Green Cabbage

Part of a traditional Southern New Year's Day, cabbage is said to provide good financial luck for the coming year.

3	slices bacon
1	large head fresh cabbage, washed, cored, and cut in bite-size chunks
1/2	large onion, thinly sliced
1	tablespoon sugar
1	tablespoon salt
1/2	teaspoon pepper
	Pickled pepper sauce (page 124) for serving (optional)

In a heavy roaster, Dutch oven, or pot, begin to fry the bacon over medium heat. When half-finished and there is oil in the pot, add the cabbage and onion, a layer at a time, over the cooking bacon, sprinkling with the sugar and salt on each layer. Continue to stir the bottom layers up from the bottom to keep from burning. The sugar and salt will begin to caramelize the cabbage and onion. Reduce the heat, cover, and allow the cabbage to wilt, stirring occasionally for about 15 minutes. Add the pepper, stir, and serve. Pass the pickled pepper sauce at the table, if desired. (Some people like to sprinkle about 1 teaspoon on top.)

Makes 6 to 8 servings

A Southern kitchen is always loud. The cooking is loud. The dish washing is loud. The conversation is loud. And the laughter is the loudest.

Catahoula Corn-Patch Corn

Corn burns easily, so stir often when on direct heat of stove.

8	ears fresh sweet corn or 1 (1-pound) package frozen cream-style corn
1	slice bacon or 1 tablespoon bacon grease
4	tablespoons butter
¼	cup heavy cream
1	teaspoon sugar
1	teaspoon salt
½	teaspoon pepper

If using fresh corn, cut the kernels off, close to the cob. Then scrape the ear to remove all the remaining milk and kernels. Heat the bacon or the bacon grease and the butter in a large cast-iron skillet. Add the corn, corn milk, and cream. Add the sugar, salt, and pepper and cook on medium heat on top of the stove, stirring often, for about 15 minutes. Preheat the oven to 450 degrees. Place the skillet in the oven for 20 to 25 minutes, stirring occasionally.

Makes 6 to 8 servings

Award-Winning Nutty-Crunch Sweet Potato Casserole

Potatoes

6	cups cooked, mashed sweet potatoes
1	cup firmly packed brown sugar
1	cup granulated sugar
2	large eggs, lightly beaten
2	teaspoons vanilla extract
2	teaspoons salt
1	teaspoon cinnamon
1	cup heavy cream
1	stick butter

Topping

1	cup firmly packed brown sugar
2/3	cup all-purpose flour
1	teaspoon salt
1	teaspoon cinnamon
1½	sticks butter, melted
2	cups chopped pecans

To make the potatoes, preheat the oven to 350 degrees. Cream together the sweet potatoes, brown sugar, granulated sugar, eggs, vanilla, salt, cinnamon, cream, and butter. Whip with a handheld electric mixer until smooth. Spread the mixture in an 11 x 9-inch glass baking dish.

To make the topping, combine all the topping ingredients in a large bowl. Sprinkle the topping on the potatoes in the baking dish. Bake for 30 to 40 minutes, or until bubbly and lightly browned.

Makes 10 to 12 servings

Just a-Swingin' Chocolate Pie

My friend, country singer John Anderson, set the musical world on its ear by topping the country charts and the pop charts in the eighties with a hit song that profiled the joys of "just a-swingin'" on the front porch with Charlotte Johnson while her brother eats homemade chocolate pie inside. It's an innocent, sweet Southern notion of courtship I'd love to bring back with this recipe. When you bake this pie, remember that even though summer nights in the South are usually hot, eggs always separate better when they are cold.

1	(9-inch) baked piecrust (page 184), not too brown
1	teaspoon powdered sugar
1	cup plus ¼ cup sugar, divided
2	tablespoons unsweetened cocoa powder
2½	tablespoons all-purpose flour
¼	teaspoon salt
2	large eggs, separated
1	cup evaporated milk
1	(1.5-ounce) Hershey's Milk Chocolate bar
1	tablespoon butter
1½	tablespoons vanilla extract
¼	teaspoon cream of tartar

Preheat the oven to 400 degrees. Sprinkle the baked piecrust with the powdered sugar to avoid a soggy crust. In a double boiler, combine 1 cup of the sugar, the cocoa powder, flour, and salt. Stir in the egg yolks and milk. Cook over medium heat. Add the chocolate bar, butter, and vanilla, stirring until the mixture becomes a thick creamy pudding. Pour the filling into the prepared piecrust and allow to set while preparing the meringue. In a clean, dry glass or metal bowl, whip the egg whites until foamy. Gradually whip in the remaining ¼ cup sugar and the cream of tartar and beat until the egg whites make stiff white peaks. Cover the filling completely with the meringue, stacking it higher in the middle. Bake for 5 to 6 minutes, or until the meringue has golden brown peaks. Chill before serving.

Makes 6 to 8 servings

Hello Dolly Bars

My mother made these every Christmas. I don't know why she didn't make them more often because they are incredibly easy. I'm probably lucky that she didn't because I'd be as big as a house. I couldn't stop eating them.

1½	sticks butter
1¼	cups graham cracker crumbs
2	cups semisweet chocolate chips
1	cup flaked coconut
1	cup chopped pecans
1	(14-ounce) can sweetened condensed milk

Preheat the oven to 350 degrees. Melt the butter and pour into a bowl. Blend in the graham cracker crumbs and pat into the bottom of a 13 x 9-inch glass baking dish to form a crust. Layer the chocolate chips evenly across the crust, followed by the coconut, then the pecans. Drizzle the condensed milk over everything, but do not mix or stir. Bake for 25 minutes on the center rack of your oven. Remove and cool before cutting into bars.

Makes 2 dozen bars

THE SILVERWARE DIDN'T ALWAYS MATCH. THE PLATES DIDN'T EITHER. THE NAPKINS WERE OFTEN FROM A PASSED-AROUND ROLL OF PAPER TOWELS. BUT THE FOOD LINGERS IN MY MIND AS THE BEST I HAVE EVER HAD IN MY LIFE, EVEN THOUGH I HAVE SAMPLED DELICACIES AT SOME OF THE FINEST RESTAURANTS IN THE WORLD.

Maw Maw's Mystery Pie

My MawMaw Cora will live in my memory as the best cook there ever was, or ever will be. She surprised me one birthday, in the dead of a wintry January, with the most delectable-tasting pie I had ever experienced. It was tropical and warm and filled with a combination of flavors that I couldn't quite put my finger on. It was better than any birthday cake I could have had. In fact, for every birthday after that, I asked for that specific pie, with a candle. When I asked her what kind of pie it was, she said she didn't know. She said it was "Misty" Pie or Mystery Pie. I didn't care, but I knew it was the best thing I'd ever tasted. I found her recipe in her Bible after she died.

1	(9-inch) unbaked piecrust (page 184)
1	teaspoon powdered sugar
1	stick butter, melted
1½	cups sugar
2¾	tablespoons all-purpose flour
4	large eggs, beaten, at room temperature
1	(8-ounce) can crushed pineapple, not drained
6	ounces grated coconut
¼	teaspoon salt
1	teaspoon vanilla extract
½	teaspoon almond extract

Preheat the oven to 350 degrees. Sprinkle the unbaked piecrust with the powdered sugar to avoid a soggy crust. In a large bowl mix together the butter, sugar, flour, eggs, pineapple, coconut, salt, vanilla, and almond extract and pour into the prepared unbaked piecrust. Bake 40 to 50 minutes, or until the top is a light golden brown.

Makes 6 to 8 servings

apple Bread

Mystery Pie

2 eggs slightly beaten
1½ cups sugar
2 Tablespoon flour
1 cup undilated Pet milk
melted

s flour sifted
Beat
sugar
king

Memories happen when I bite into a recipe
that I know was my grandmother's.
I remember her hands . . .
arthritis, age spots, and reddened skin
from years of washing dishes by hand, and a
simple wedding ring that she never took off her finger.

1½ cups flour
1½ teaspoon sugar
1 teas salt
½ cups cook oil
cold milk

Butter-Maple Pecan Pie

This is an amazing dessert served warm with vanilla ice cream!

1	stick butter
3/4	cup light corn syrup (such as Karo)
1/4	cup maple syrup
3/4	cup granulated sugar
1/4	cup firmly packed light brown sugar
2	tablespoons all-purpose flour
3	large eggs, beaten
1/2	teaspoon lemon juice
1	teaspoon vanilla extract
1	teaspoon almond extract
1/2	teaspoon salt
1 1/2	cups chopped pecans
1	(9-inch) unbaked piecrust (page 184)

Preheat the oven to 425 degrees. Brown the butter in a heavy skillet until golden brown (be careful not to burn it). Remove the butter from the burner and let cool. In a medium bowl combine the corn syrup, maple syrup, granulated sugar, brown sugar, flour, eggs, lemon juice, vanilla extract, almond extract, salt, and pecans. Blend well and stir in the melted butter. Pour into the unbaked piecrust and bake on the top rack in the center of the oven at 425 degrees for 10 minutes. Reduce the baking temperature to 325 degrees and continue to bake for 40 minutes. Let cool before serving.

Makes 6 to 8 servings

No *S*unday dinner is complete in the South *without dessert.*

Don't let anyone fool you.
Home in the South is where the food is.

Biscuits, Country Ham, and Grits

Breakfast in the South

Breakfast in the South sets the tone for the day. It's the scent that lingers. It's the bacon grease for the rest of the meals. It's biscuits to put in your pocket for later. It's a Bible verse read before grace. It's accompanied by the ancient sound of a Big Ben clock and a crowing rooster. Plans are made, prayers are said, and promises are kept. It's robust and fresh and never seems hurried. Breakfast in the South, like many things, stays with you.

Self-Rising Biscuits

This recipe is very old. As my mother read the ingredients to me, she reminded me that the old wives' kitchen tip about biscuits was, "Cook 'em real hot and real fast."

2	**cups self-rising flour**
¼	**cup butter-flavored shortening**
¾	**cup milk**

Preheat the oven to 500 degrees. Sift the flour into a bowl and cut in the shortening with a pastry cutter until the mixture is the consistency of fine cornmeal. Add the milk very gradually, working the mixture into a soft dough. Turn out on a floured surface and knead for "about half a minute." (This was actually written in the old recipe that was in my grandmother's kitchen.) Roll the dough out to a ½-inch thickness and cut with a biscuit cutter. Place the biscuits on a greased biscuit pan and bake for about 10 minutes.

Makes 10 to 12 biscuits

Mayonnaise Muffins

1	**cup self-rising flour**
1	**tablespoon mayonnaise**
2	**tablespoons sugar**
1/8	**teaspoon salt**
1/2	**cup half-and-half**
	Nonstick cooking spray

Preheat the oven to 350 degrees. In a medium bowl gently blend, but do not beat, the flour, mayonnaise, sugar, salt, and half-and-half. Spray 6 muffin cups with nonstick cooking spray and fill each half full of batter. Bake for 10 to 15 minutes, or until golden brown.

Makes 6 muffins

My mother never rolled out and cut biscuits in her life. She was the big drop-biscuit queen. She'd drop the biscuits on a pan poured with oil, turning over each dollop of dough in the oil, so they were shiny and saturated before baking. The biscuits would be lightly crunchy on the outside and buttery fluff on the inside. Filled with homemade mayhaw jelly, *these biscuits were the reason to get up early on a Saturday, even when you could sleep in.*

Pumpkin Bread

Served warm, this is a great excuse for honey-walnut cream cheese, spread on thick, with a hot, strong cup of Community brand coffee, a dark Louisiana brand that finally is available in most major grocery stores. I used to bring back pounds of it from trips home and keep it in my freezer, just to keep from getting homesick.

1²/₃	**cups all-purpose flour**
1¼	**cups sugar**
¼	**cup firmly packed dark brown sugar**
1	**teaspoon baking soda**
¼	**teaspoon baking powder**
¼	**tablespoon salt**
2	**cups pureed pumpkin (canned is fine)**
1	**tablespoon pumpkin pie spice**
2	**large eggs**
¼	**cup vegetable oil**
¼	**cup applesauce**
¼	**cup vanilla yogurt**
¼	**cup water**
½	**cup chopped walnuts**

Preheat the oven to 350 degrees. Grease and flour two 8 x 4 x 3-inch loaf pans. In a large bowl blend all the ingredients. Pour into the prepared pans and bake for 1½ hours.

Makes 16 servings

There is comfort in making food that reminds you of *H*ome.

Use-Up-the-Brown-Bananas Bread

My dad's favorite cake, bread, cupcake, or dessert was banana bread. We constantly tried to create the perfect recipe. Beautiful bananas meant a packed, flat cake that didn't rise. Yuck. Green bananas were even worse. But oddly enough, when the bananas looked their worst, the banana bread was at its best. This is my favorite way to get potassium!

1	cup sugar
½	cup shortening
2	large eggs
3	very ripe large bananas, peeled and crushed
2	cups all-purpose flour
1	teaspoon baking soda
2	teaspoons vanilla extract
½	cup chopped walnuts or other nuts
1	cup raisins or chopped dates (optional)

Preheat the oven to 375 degrees. Grease and flour a 9-inch loaf pan. Cream together the sugar and shortening and add the eggs, one at a time, beating for 30 seconds after each addition. Alternately add the bananas with the flour, baking soda, and vanilla and mix at low speed with a handheld electric mixer for about 15 seconds. Add the nuts and raisins or dates, if desired, and blend gently. Pour into the prepared pan and bake for 45 minutes, or until a toothpick inserted in the middle of the bread comes out clean.

Makes 8 servings

Monkey Bread

A Southern lady is always prepared to entertain, and I was taught that canned biscuits could be an integral part of that magic. From pizza crust to homemade cinnamon rolls to dumplings, a can of biscuits can save the day. They also make the same sound when you open them as taking off your girdle at the end of a long day.

4	cups sugar
2	tablespoons cinnamon
4	(8-count) cans regular-size butter-flaky layered refrigerated biscuits
1½	sticks butter
1¼	cups firmly packed light brown sugar

Preheat the oven to 350 degrees. Grease a 9-inch loaf pan or baking dish. In a large zip-top bag, make a dredge out of the 4 cups sugar and the cinnamon. Cut each biscuit into quarters and shake them in the bag, covering them with the sweet mix. Begin layering the biscuit puffs in the prepared baking dish. Repeat the dredge and layer until all the biscuits are used and layered and the loaf pan is full. Push down the layers so they stick together and all the biscuit puffs fit in the loaf pan. In a small saucepan melt the butter and brown sugar and let it boil for no longer than 1 minute, stirring constantly. Pour the mixture over the sugared biscuit layers and bake for 35 minutes. Turn out on a platter and either cut or pull apart for an easy coffee cake that kids love to help make and eat!

Makes 8 to 10 servings

Monkey Bread Dip

Monkey Bread is just fine served "plain," if you can call brown sugar, cinnamon, and melted-butter glaze plain. But since everything is great with cream cheese icing, this recipe can be served in individual ramekins like butter for an extra treat.

1½   **(8-ounce) packages cream cheese, softened**
3   **sticks butter, softened**
¼   **cup powdered sugar**
1½   **teaspoons vanilla extract**
1   **teaspoon lemon juice**

In a medium bowl whip together the cream cheese and butter with a handheld electric mixer and then slowly add the powdered sugar, continuing to blend with the mixer for at least 10 minutes. Add the vanilla, continuing to mix. Add the lemon juice, continuing to mix until the icing is creamy. Frost when the bread is cooled, or serve as a dip when the bread is warm.

Makes 2 cups

Apple-Nut Loaf

Cake

1	cup sugar
¼	cup butter-flavored shortening
¼	cup applesauce
2	large eggs
2	cups all-purpose flour
1	teaspoon baking soda
¼	teaspoon salt
2	tablespoons vanilla yogurt
1	tablespoon vanilla extract
1	cup chopped walnuts
1	cup peeled and grated apples

Topping

2	tablespoons sugar
½	teaspoon cinnamon
½	teaspoon dark brown sugar
¼	teaspoon salt
¼	cup very finely chopped pecans
2	tablespoons butter

To make the cake, preheat the oven to 350 degrees. Grease and flour a 9 x 5 x 3-inch loaf pan. In a large bowl combine the sugar, shortening, and applesauce, mixing until creamy. Add the eggs, one at a time, and beat the mixture well after each addition. In a medium bowl sift the flour, baking soda, and salt. In a small bowl blend the yogurt and vanilla. Add the dry mixture and yogurt mixture alternately to the creamy mixture, beating well after each addition. Stir in the walnuts and apples, and when well mixed, pour the batter into the prepared pan.

To make the topping, combine all the topping ingredients in a small bowl. Sprinkle the topping on the loaf and dot with butter. Bake for 1 hour. Allow the loaf to cool for at least 10 minutes before turning out on a serving plate. This loaf is delicious by itself or spread with softened cream cheese or honey butter.

Makes 8 servings

OUR MUFFINS WERE MADE WITH BLUEBERRIES PICKED RIGHT OFF BUSHES IN THE FRONT YARD. THAT LOUISIANA SOIL GREW THEM ALMOST AS BIG AS GRAPES. T WAS IMPOSSIBLE TO TAKE A BITE OF A MUFFIN AND NOT GET SOME BERRY.

Peanut Butter Muffins

My great granny Walker, "Maw" as we called her, used to keep her pantry stocked with peanut butter and vanilla wafers. I can't think of her without thinking of those two things. Those were simple times, and these muffins remind me of that simplicity, served warm with cream cheese or peanut butter spread.

1/3	cup butter-flavored shortening
1 1/2	cups firmly packed brown sugar, divided
1/2	teaspoon salt
1	teaspoon vanilla extract
1/2	cup peanut butter
2	large eggs, beaten
2 1/2	teaspoons baking powder
2	cups all-purpose flour
3/4	cup milk

Preheat the oven to 350 degrees. Grease a muffin tin. Place the shortening in a large bowl. Gradually add 1 cup of the brown sugar, the salt, and the vanilla, and cream together until fluffy. Add the peanut butter, continuing to blend. Set aside. In another bowl, beat the eggs well. Add the remaining 1/2 cup brown sugar and mix until completely blended. Stir into the creamed mixture gradually until completely blended. In another bowl, sift together the baking powder and flour. Gradually add the dry ingredients and the milk alternately to the creamed mixture, mixing well after each addition. Pour into the prepared muffin tin and bake for 25 to 30 minutes.

Makes 1 dozen muffins

Hidden-Layer Sour Cream– Pecan Coffee Cake

Imagine a coffee cake with a topping in the middle as well as on top. If that sounds tasty, you'll love this recipe. It's easy, freezable, and perfect for taking to a ladies' tea or to the office during the holidays. This recipe is easily seventy years old, with a few of my additions.

Cake

4	tablespoons butter
1	cup sugar
2	large eggs
2	cups all-purpose flour
1	teaspoon baking powder
1	teaspoon baking soda
½	teaspoon salt
1	cup sour cream
1	teaspoon vanilla extract

Topping

1	cup firmly packed dark brown sugar
½	cup finely chopped pecans
3	tablespoons all-purpose flour
2	teaspoons ground cinnamon
3	tablespoons butter, softened

To make the cake, preheat the oven to 375 degrees. Grease a 9-inch square baking pan. In a large bowl cream the butter and sugar until the mixture is light and fluffy. Add the eggs, one at a time, and blend well after each addition. In another bowl sift the flour with the baking powder, baking soda, and salt. Add the dry ingredients to the creamed mixture, alternating with the sour cream. Beat well after each addition. Add the vanilla, stirring well.

To make the topping, in a small bowl stir together all the topping ingredients with a fork until the mixture is crumbly. Pour half the cake batter into the prepared pan. Sprinkle with half the topping. Add the remaining batter and sprinkle with the remaining topping. Bake for 35 minutes, or until a toothpick inserted in the middle of the cake comes out clean.

Makes 8 servings

Baking and sifting go together, *or at least that's what my mother said, and her mother before her, and my home economics teacher. Even though most flours today are presifted, in baking, the sifting adds air to flour, making a lighter cake. If you are blending dry ingredients, you should sift them together to make sure all the spices are blended in equally, as in the Honey Boys recipe on page 110.* Will it ruin your recipe if you don't sift? *Probably not, but sifting might just make it better!*

Strawberry Breakfast Spread

2   **sticks butter**
½   **(8-ounce) package cream cheese, softened**
½   **cup chopped fresh strawberries**
2   **tablespoons powdered sugar**

In a medium bowl cream together the butter, cream cheese, strawberries, and powdered sugar until well blended. Cover the container and allow the spread to chill overnight. Remove the spread from the refrigerator at least 15 minutes prior to serving. Serve with hot biscuits, warm bagels, breakfast rolls, or scones.

Makes enough spread for 8 to 10 biscuits

Sunday Morning Waffles

This is a tasty variation on an old theme. Waffle batter can also be refrigerated for later use if there are any leftovers. Try setting up a waffle bar with fresh fruits, nuts, flavored butters, and syrups to offer a warm welcome to overnight guests. Waffle bars are easy and fun, and children can even join in.

1¾	**cups all-purpose flour**
3	**tablespoons sugar**
½	**teaspoon salt**
½	**teaspoon cinnamon**
1	**tablespoon baking powder**
2	**large eggs**
1¾	**cups milk**
1	**stick butter, melted**
½	**teaspoon vanilla extract**
½	**teaspoon almond extract**
	Nonstick cooking spray

In a large bowl combine the flour, sugar, salt, cinnamon, and baking powder. In another bowl whisk together the eggs, milk, butter, vanilla extract, and almond extract. Stir the dry ingredients into the liquid and stir until well blended. Pour onto a preheated waffle iron that has been sprayed with nonstick cooking spray. Cook the waffles for about 3 minutes, or until they are lightly golden with a touch of crunch.

Makes about 9 (4½-inch) square waffles

Cecil Ray's Bacon Waffles

Cecil Ray Johnston was married to Juanita Johnston for more than sixty years. He didn't cook much, except on Sunday when he always made waffles, and these were his specialties. He'd keep asking if you wanted another, a half, a quarter, no matter what you said, and he always made one extra plain waffle for the birds. Cecil Ray always liked his waffles topped with molasses. I prefer maple syrup with mine.

	Nonstick cooking spray
4	**slices bacon, cut in half**
1	**recipe waffle batter (from master mix on page 8 or Sunday Morning Waffles on page 43)**

Preheat the waffle iron, spray with nonstick cooking spray, and place 1 half slice of bacon on each waffle square. Close the waffle iron and allow the bacon to cook through but remain flexible, about 2 to 3 minutes. Open the waffle iron and pour the batter over the bacon, allowing the batter to enclose each slice. Cook the waffles until done, about 2 minutes, and serve hot with the syrup of your choice.

Makes 8 (4½-inch) square waffles

Bacon is always where you start. *It's the foundation of everything Southern. It's in your pole beans, your cornbread, your first homegrown-tomato BLT, and it's the smell that always reminds me of home.* **It's smoky, salty, and the distinct flavor of the South.**

There is nothing more gratifying than finding your first egg from chickens you've raised. It shines there like a toasty brown beacon of accomplishment. I'm not sure who was prouder—me or the chicken.

New Orleans Egg Scramble

One of my favorite things is re-creating especially wonderful meals I experience in restaurants. Sometimes I get close, sometimes I'm right on the money, and sometimes I just book reservations again at the same restaurant. This is one of the best breakfasts I ever had in New Orleans. I got very, very close on this one.

10	large eggs
1	teaspoon salt
½	teaspoon pepper
½	cup chopped chives
½	cup milk
2	tablespoons butter
½	(8-ounce) package cream cheese, cubed

In a medium bowl whisk together the eggs, salt, pepper, chives, and milk. Melt the butter in a heated skillet and then add the egg mixture. Scramble until the eggs are almost completely firm, and then equally distribute the cubed cream cheese and integrate into the eggs. When the cream cheese is warm, just beginning to melt, and the eggs are firm, serve immediately.

Makes 4 to 5 servings

I knew I was no longer in the South when they had never heard of grits and all the tea was unsweetened.

Good Grits Casserole

4	cups water
1/2	teaspoon Cajun seasoning
1¼	cups quick-cooking grits
1	cup grated sharp Cheddar cheese, divided
4	slices American cheese
4	tablespoons butter
5	large eggs, beaten
1	cup milk
1	pound ground sausage, cooked and drained

Preheat the oven to 350 degrees. Grease a 13 x 9-inch casserole dish. In a large pot bring the water and Cajun seasoning to a boil. Add the grits slowly, stirring until there are no lumps. Reduce the heat and allow the grits to cook for 5 minutes. Remove the grits from the heat. Stir in 3/4 cup of the Cheddar cheese, the American cheese slices, and the butter and allow these ingredients to melt. Stir in the beaten eggs and milk and pour the mixture into the prepared baking dish. Top the grits and eggs mixture with the sausage and the remaining 1/4 cup Cheddar cheese. Bake the casserole for 1 hour. Allow the dish to cool for 5 to 10 minutes before serving warm.

Makes 6 to 8 servings

Brunch Pasta

For those days when you sleep in and want eggs and bacon, but it's later in the day and you want a meal to keep you full for two meals, this is a perfect dish. It's easy, filling, and quite impressive for overnight guests. The Italians make a dish called pasta carbonara. This is based on that dish, with a Southern touch.

3	tablespoons olive oil
1	(12-ounce) package penne pasta, cooked al dente
6	large eggs
2	slices American cheese
1	cup shredded Parmesan cheese, divided
6	slices bacon, fried and crumbled
1/2	teaspoon garlic powder
1/2	teaspoon salt
1/2	teaspoon pepper

In a large skillet or frying pan, heat the oil and add the cooked pasta. Quickly crack the eggs evenly in the pan and begin to scramble with the pasta. Add the American cheese, 1/2 cup of the Parmesan cheese, and the bacon, and integrate it into the pasta as the cheeses begin to melt. Gently blend in the garlic powder, salt, and pepper and serve immediately, topping each serving with the remaining 1/2 cup Parmesan cheese.

Makes 4 servings

Egg Toast and Fried Apple-Pecan Compote

This was a special treat my family enjoyed on Saturdays. We didn't have to go anywhere that day, so we luxuriated in making and eating egg toast and bacon. This "toast" tastes much like egg custard and bread pudding all in one. I make the compote prior to the egg toast so it can be cooking and soaking up the flavors while I prepare the toast. A side of fried apples and pecans just adds to the joy!

Compote

4	tablespoons butter
6	medium apples, peeled and sliced
½	cup firmly packed brown sugar
½	teaspoon cinnamon
½	cup chopped pecans
⅛	teaspoon salt
½	cup water

Egg Toast

4	tablespoons butter
3	large eggs, beaten
¼	cup milk (or evaporated milk, for added richness)
1	teaspoon vanilla extract
½	teaspoon cinnamon
¼	teaspoon nutmeg
½	teaspoon salt
1	teaspoon sugar
8	bread slices (any loaf bread will do)

To make the compote, melt the butter in a medium skillet, and stir-fry the apples, brown sugar, cinnamon, pecans, and salt until the apples are tender, about 15 minutes. Add the water as the syrup thickens and stir all the sugar away from the bottom and sides of the pan. Serve as a complement to the egg toast with bacon or crumbled bacon on top.

To make the egg toast, heat the butter in a large skillet and allow it to melt over medium-high heat. Meanwhile, in a medium bowl, whisk together the eggs, milk, vanilla, cinnamon, nutmeg, salt, and sugar. Submerge each bread slice in the egg mixture, just long enough to coat both sides in the egg mixture but not to saturate the bread. Place the coated bread in the hot skillet and cook each side until lightly browned, about 2 minutes on each side. Transfer to a warming plate until all pieces are cooked. Serve warm. Use additional butter in the skillet if the toast begins to stick.

Makes 8 servings

My grandfather grew sugarcane just so we could have our own homegrown cane syrup. The cane was cultivated and cut, and we'd always get some raw cane to chew on during the process. The stalks were pressed and the juice was boiled, as the cane was made into syrup in a tedious process. I tasted some of the cane juice at different parts of the process, which I don't recommend. Cane juice isn't spectacular. But at the end of the process, the dark brown slow-moving syrup, strong in flavor and filled with nutrients, became **something I *craved* on a biscuit, pancakes, or even a peanut butter sandwich.**

Christmas Morning Casserole

This easy make-ahead breakfast casserole is perfect for those early see-what-Santa-Claus-brought mornings when you don't want to cook but you are starving. With Christmas dinner to prepare, and the joy of opening those early presents, you simply stick this casserole in to bake. It's great for overnight guest breakfasts, Sunday school brunches, and breakfast meetings.

1	pound ground sausage
4	tablespoons butter
6	slices potato bread, no crust (Give the crusts to the birds. They're hungry this time of year!)
2	cups shredded mild Cheddar cheese
8	large eggs, beaten
2	cups milk
1½	teaspoons seasoning salt

Cook the sausage and drain. Melt the butter in a 13 x 9-inch baking dish. Line the baking dish with the potato bread slices, over the melted butter. Layer the cooked sausage over the potato bread. Layer the cheese over the sausage. In a large bowl beat the eggs, milk, and seasoning salt together. Pour the egg mixture over the entire contents of the baking dish. Cover and refrigerate overnight.

The next day, preheat the oven to 350 degrees and bake the casserole for 45 minutes.

Makes 6 to 8 servings

Broiler Bacon

Frying bacon in a big black skillet was how I learned. But when a friend showed me how to do bacon in the oven, it made life a lot easier.

12 slices bacon

Preheat the broiler (about 450 degrees). Lay the bacon strips on a broiler pan or a baking pan (making sure that the bacon grease has somewhere to drain, or an edge on the pan that can keep the grease from pouring out of the pan into the oven). When the broiler is preheated, place the bacon pan under the broiler for 3 to 6 minutes. Keep a close check on the bacon because it can burn easily. When done, carefully remove the pan from the oven, and use tongs to move the bacon to a platter lined with a paper towel to remove excess grease. You will have perfect bacon, just like restaurants serve. Don't forget to pour the bacon grease left over in the pan into a jar or reservoir for use in other recipes.

Makes 6 servings

Kentucky Country Ham and Red-Eye Gravy

One of the best things about country ham is the salty, smoky taste that just goes great on a biscuit. This recipe is said to have come about when workmen or hunters around a campfire cooked their salt-meat for breakfast. They just poured their extra coffee in the drippings to make gravy. The water in the coffee made little "red eyes" in the fat left in the skillet, and oh what wonderful gravy!

8	**serving portions country ham, sliced about ¼ inch thick**
2	**tablespoons vegetable oil**
2	**teaspoons sugar (brown sugar will work too), divided**
1	**cup strong black coffee (can be left over from the day before)**
½	**cup water**

Cut the ham into serving slices while heating the oil in a skillet on medium-high. Add the ham to the hot skillet and cook for about 8 minutes on each side. Before you turn the ham, sprinkle with half the sugar. Sprinkle the other side with sugar once cooked. Pour in the coffee and water, and stir to make gravy around the meat. Reduce the heat, cover, and allow to slow simmer for 5 to 10 minutes.

Makes 8 servings

One thing to remember: *Never take country ham biscuits on a walk in the woods for a snack, unless you are ready to carry three gallons of water.* My dad made that mistake when he was a young man heading out to his deer stand for a hunt. An hour later he was so thirsty, he was looking for puddles that were clear enough to drink from.

Sausage Cream Gravy

A meal in itself over a hot buttermilk biscuit, sausage and gravy tops the list of "foods that make you homesick" for transplanted Southerners.

1	**pound ground pork sausage**
4	**tablespoons all-purpose flour**
2	**cups hot milk**
1	**teaspoon salt**
1	**teaspoon pepper**
⅛	**teaspoon Tabasco sauce**

Cook the sausage in a large skillet until browned, making sure to break up the meat as it cooks. Transfer with a slotted spoon or strainer to a paper towel, leaving the pan drippings. Stir the flour into the hot grease, stirring constantly and scraping the skillet of any residue. (Everything is part of the gravy.) Cook and stir for about 2 minutes. Heat the milk in the microwave for 1 minute, or bring just to a boil in a saucepan on the stove. Add the hot milk, stirring the gravy until creamy and blended. Add the salt, pepper, and Tabasco sauce, continuing to stir and cook for about 5 minutes. If the gravy seems too thick, add more hot milk, and keep stirring. Add the crumbled sausage to the gravy, stirring it so that it will heat through. Serve immediately over hot biscuits, grits, fried potatoes, or cornbread, or sneak some just by itself!

Makes about 4 cups

Fried Bologna-Egg Sandwich

I heard a news story once about two fugitives who escaped from the Tennessee Department of Corrections because they were craving a fried "baloney" sandwich from a little-known diner in Bucksnort, Tennessee. Now, that must have been some sandwich, because they were apprehended and back in custody before nightfall, but not until they'd been satiated with one of life's simple pleasures, a thick-sliced fried bologna sandwich. This recipe joins two lowly comfort foods in one delectable combo that whistles "Dixie" with every bite. The outside is lightly crisped like a grilled cheese sandwich, and the inside is filled with a breakfast that will hold you all day.

2	tablespoons butter
2	large eggs
2	thick slices bologna, each slice cut from center to edge to prevent puffing up
4	slices white bread, buttered on one side
2	slices American cheese
1/8	teaspoon salt
1/8	teaspoon pepper
	Mayonnaise (optional)

In a medium skillet over medium-high heat, melt the butter and begin frying the eggs. In another preheated skillet, sear the bologna until it browns on one side, and then quickly turn and repeat on the other side. Flip the eggs, as you toast the four pieces of bread, butter sides down, in a third skillet or on a griddle. Place the bologna on two of the upturned pieces of bread. Place a slice of cheese on each and when the yolks are completely cooked, remove the fried eggs and place one egg on top of each cheese slice. Dust with salt and pepper and top with the other pieces of toasted bread. Add a thin layer of mayonnaise to the sandwich, if desired.

Makes 2 sandwiches

I was ten years old and I couldn't see over the big black cast-iron skillet. So Mom made me pull up a chair, a burnt orange floral Naugahyde chair from the kitchen dinette. She laid the greasy strips of raw bacon neatly in rows as the skillet heated. Gradually the fat began turning from creamy white to amber translucence as

I came of age as a woman
in the Southern kitchen.

Homegrown Tomatoes and Fresh Corn
Treasures from the Southern Garden

No one sees anything missing when there is a bountiful harvest of fresh vegetables and fruits on the Southern table. There's never a "where's the meat?" comment. Ladies and gentlemen, rich folks and not so rich, saints and hellions, all connect with the earth and her bounty come springtime in the South. The garden is a hobby for some, a necessity for others. Fruit trees bloom abundantly and pecan orchards litter the ground with plantations of goodness that fill the world's need for delicious desserts. No matter what incredible dishes are created in the Southern kitchen, every one of them is better when accompanied by the words "from my garden."

Frozen Strawberry Jam

My mother made this recipe one year because of the bumper crop of strawberries on our patio. It was bright, fresh, and delicious, and even in the middle of winter, it was like a garden-sweet moment. This recipe is great on hot biscuits and luscious on vanilla ice cream.

4	cups crushed strawberries (from 2 quarts whole berries)
2	(3.5-ounce) boxes fruit pectin
1	cup light corn syrup (such as Karo)
5	cups sugar
¼	cup lemon juice (for color)

Place the crushed strawberries in a bowl. Sift in the fruit pectin, stirring vigorously, and allow to set for 30 minutes, stirring occasionally. Add the corn syrup and mix well, and then stir in the sugar until it's dissolved. Stir in the lemon juice, and when the jam is well blended, pour into sterile jars and fill to ¼ inch from the top, sealing with boiled lids. Store in the freezer. Return to the freezer after serving. This jam remains "dippable" even when frozen.

Makes 6 pints

Southern food begins with what's fresh and in season, or what you or someone you know has put up in the freezer or the pantry when it was fresh and in season.

Pear Honey

In the South, many recipes have come from using what many would throw away. Sometimes the best flavor comes from the peelings of the fruits, so many preserves will contain them. Although the clear juice is strained in this recipe, the peelings are still used.

16	**large pears**
4	**cups sugar**
	Juice from 1 lemon

Peel and slice the pears, discarding the stems and hard cores. In a large stockpot cover the peelings and fruit with just enough water to touch the edge of the top of the fruit. Boil the fruit and peelings, stirring and pressing down on the fruit as it cooks. When the peelings are completely limp and the fruit is cooked until it becomes a mush, strain the juice through cheesecloth to get 8 cups. Using the same stockpot, boil the juice vigorously with the sugar and lemon juice. Continue to boil until the juice reduces to a honey consistency. Pour into hot sterile jars to ¼ inch from the top and seal with boiled lids. The jars can be stored, unrefrigerated, in a cabinet or pantry for 2 years, as long as the jars remain unopened and the lids remain sealed. Once opened, refrigerate. This recipe can easily be reduced to 8 pears, 4 cups juice, 2 cups sugar, and juice from half a lemon to yield 1 pint of honey.

Makes 2 pints

Frozen Strawberry Salad

If you attend a women's event in the South, be it church related, social, or simply a girls' gathering, there will be an offering of congealed salad, humble and deliciously Southern.

2   cups frozen strawberries, with juice
2   large bananas, chopped
1   teaspoon lemon juice
1   (20-ounce) can crushed pineapple, drained
1   cup sugar
1   (8-ounce) container frozen whipped topping, thawed
1   (8-ounce) package cream cheese, softened

Blend the berries, bananas, lemon juice, pineapple, and sugar in a blender. Pour the fruit mixture into a large bowl. Stir in the whipped topping. Whip in the cream cheese with a handheld electric mixer. Spread into a 13 x 9-inch Pyrex dish, cover, and freeze. These are lovely garnished with fresh strawberry slices and served on baby lettuce leaves.

Makes 12 servings

Honey-Fried Apples

3	**large apples**
4	**tablespoons butter**
3	**tablespoons brown sugar**
1	**teaspoon cinnamon**
¼	**cup sugar**
2	**tablespoons honey**
¼	**teaspoon nutmeg**
¼	**teaspoon salt**
¼	**cup water**

Core and slice the apples as you melt the butter in a large skillet. Layer the apple slices in the skillet, sprinkling the layers with brown sugar. Cook over medium heat. Continue to stir the apples and gradually stir in the cinnamon, sugar, honey, nutmeg, salt, and water, making sure that all the sugar is dissolved. Reduce the heat, cover, and simmer until the apples are tender, 15 to 20 minutes. Serve hot. For an interesting taste combination, try this recipe with 4 tablespoons bacon grease instead of butter.

Makes 4 servings

ANYTHING that came out of the garden was fare for a meal.

We didn't just experience meat and three—we experienced meat and whatever made the table look full.

Garden-Fresh Quiche

3	large eggs, beaten
1	(8-ounce) package cream cheese
1/4	cup heavy cream
2	tablespoons all-purpose flour
1/2	cup peeled, chopped, and seeded tomato
1/2	cup finely chopped green onions
1/4	cup frozen green peas
1/4	cup grated carrot
1	teaspoon salt
1/8	teaspoon dried basil
1/2	teaspoon pepper
1/4	cup grated Jarlsberg cheese
1	(9-inch) unbaked deep-dish piecrust (page 184)
1/4	cup grated sharp Cheddar cheese

Preheat the oven to 350 degrees. In a large bowl beat the eggs, cream cheese, and cream together with a handheld electric mixer until smooth. Gradually add the flour and whip until blended. Fold in the tomato, green onions, green peas, and carrot, one at a time, and then fold in the salt, basil, and pepper. Add the Jarlsberg cheese and pour the mixture into the piecrust, topping with the Cheddar cheese. Bake for 25 minutes, or until the top is a golden bubbly delight. Remove the quiche from the oven and allow it to cool for about 5 minutes before cutting and serving.

Makes 6 servings

Garden Gumbo

This is also a great recipe to make with all the leftover veggies from the week. The okra thickens this vegetable stew, which is wonderful served hot with cornbread right out of the oven, either buttered or crumbled in the gumbo.

4	cups chicken broth
2	(16-ounce) packages frozen soup mix vegetables with okra
2	cups peeled, chopped potatoes
3	large carrots, peeled and sliced
1	stalk celery, chopped
1	large onion, chopped
2	(15-ounce) cans stewed tomatoes, including juice
1	(11-ounce) can whole-kernel corn
1	teaspoon salt
1	teaspoon pepper
½	teaspoon Cajun seasoning

In a large saucepan combine all the ingredients. Bring to a boil and then cover, reduce the heat, and cook for about 30 minutes, or until the vegetables are tender.

Makes 8 servings

We'd share our bounty with everyone from neighbors to family to the entire church membership. Others had gardens and did the same. *I can remember Sundays when the fellowship hall of the church smelled like a farmer's market.*

Simple Feel-Better Soup

Whenever I was sick, my sweet neighbor Ruth Passons would make this simple soup, and I promise you, it has magical healing powers! If I am congested, I even add ½ teaspoon minced garlic and ½ teaspoon Tabasco sauce.

1	(15-ounce) can stewed tomatoes, diced
1	cup chicken broth
1	cup peeled, chopped potatoes
1	medium onion, chopped
1	cup baby carrots
½	teaspoon salt
½	teaspoon pepper

In a large saucepan bring all the ingredients to a boil. Reduce the heat, cover, and simmer until the potatoes and carrots are tender. Serve hot.

Makes 4 servings

Creamy Corn Chowder

I began throwing things together one night and came up with a comfort soup that is wonderful with muffins and a salad or perfect as a hearty meal in itself.

2	cups fresh whole-kernel sweet corn, cut from the cob
2	cups peeled, cubed medium potatoes
1	large red bell pepper, chopped
1	large green bell pepper, chopped
1	large sweet onion, chopped
1	teaspoon salt
1	teaspoon pepper
1/2	teaspoon minced garlic
3/4	teaspoon chopped fresh basil or crushed dried basil
2	cups chicken or vegetable broth
1	cup milk
1	cup heavy cream
6	slices bacon, fried and crumbled

In a large soup pot bring the corn, potatoes, bell peppers, onion, salt, pepper, garlic, basil, broth, and milk to a boil. Reduce the temperature to medium and simmer for 15 to 20 minutes, or until the vegetables are just tender. Stir occasionally to avoid sticking and to fully integrate the flavors. When the onions are clear and the potatoes are tender, reduce the heat to warm and stir in the heavy cream. Serve hot, garnished with crumbled bacon.

Makes 8 servings

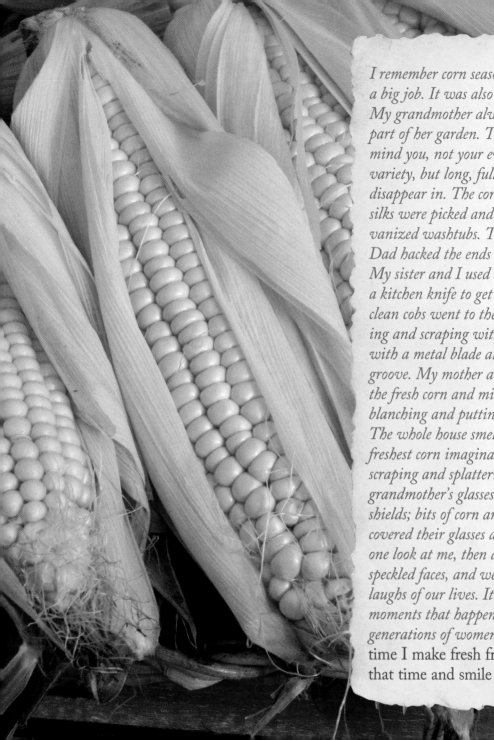

I remember corn season for our family was a big job. It was also one of my favorites! My grandmother always planted the corn in part of her garden. The garden was huge— mind you, not your everyday sort of backyard variety, but long, full rows that you could disappear in. The corn and its long golden silks were picked and piled high in big galvanized washtubs. The assembly line began. Dad hacked the ends off with a meat cleaver. My sister and I used an old toothbrush and a kitchen knife to get the silks off. Then the clean cobs went to the sink inside for washing and scraping with this long wooden tool with a metal blade at the end of a cob-shaped groove. My mother and grandmother scraped the fresh corn and milk into big dishpans for blanching and putting up in freezer bags. The whole house smelled like the sweetest, freshest corn imaginable. But with all the scraping and splattering, my mother's and grandmother's glasses looked like dirty windshields; bits of corn and white creamy residue covered their glasses and faces. They took one look at me, then at each other with their speckled faces, and we all had one of the best laughs of our lives. It was one of those special moments that happen once in a lifetime, three generations of women united in "corn." Every time I make fresh fried corn, I remember that time and smile all over again.

Corn Chow-Chow

Chow-chow is a relish that is served as a condiment with meats, beans, peas, or vegetables, or offered as a dip for chips. It's a salty-sweet mix that adds a kick to almost anything.

2	cups fresh whole-kernel sweet corn, cut from the cob
¼	cup finely chopped green bell pepper
¼	cup finely chopped red bell pepper
¼	cup cooked black beans, drained
½	medium onion, minced
1	stalk celery, peeled and finely chopped
1	teaspoon salt
¼	teaspoon dry mustard
2	tablespoons sugar
3	tablespoons apple cider vinegar
1	tablespoon olive oil
½	teaspoon cayenne pepper
½	teaspoon minced garlic

Combine all the ingredients in a saucepan over medium heat and simmer for 10 minutes. Remove from the heat, transfer to a bowl or container, cover, and refrigerate overnight. Serve cold.

Makes 3 cups

Green Pea Salad

4	cups frozen green peas, thawed
1	large egg, hard-boiled and chopped
2	tablespoons Miracle Whip
1	tablespoon minced onion
1	teaspoon minced garlic
¼	cup crumbled fried bacon
1	tablespoon honey-mustard dressing
½	teaspoon salt
½	teaspoon pepper
⅛	teaspoon cayenne pepper
½	cup shredded sharp Cheddar cheese

In a medium bowl combine all the ingredients. Cover and refrigerate for 1 hour before serving.

Makes 6 servings

The South is sweet, polite, and overly generous when it comes to food. But never turn your nose up at something someone's slaved over in the kitchen. Not only is it considered bad manners, but you'll be talked about behind your back until you die.

Sour Cream Potato Salad

4	large eggs, hard-boiled
2/3	cup Miracle Whip
3/4	cup sour cream
1	teaspoon brown prepared mustard
1/2	teaspoon horseradish
7	medium potatoes, peeled, boiled until just tender, and cubed
1/3	cup finely chopped sweet onion
1/3	cup Italian salad dressing
1	teaspoon salt
1	teaspoon pepper
1/2	teaspoon minced garlic
1/2	pound bacon, fried crisp and crumbled

Cut the eggs in half, removing the cooked yolks. In a small bowl mash the yolks with the Miracle Whip, sour cream, mustard, and horseradish. Chop the egg whites and blend in a large bowl with the potatoes, onion, and Italian dressing. Fold in the mayonnaise mixture and blend in the salt, pepper, and garlic. Cover the salad and chill overnight. Just prior to serving, stir the salad and top with the bacon.

Makes 8 servings

Nonnie's Nine-Day Slaw

There are a lot of wonderful people in the South. They are good to others, raise good kids, and do lots of good things that no one will ever know about. They never become famous. They seldom become rich. Sometimes the only legacy they leave is an adoring family, a serving dish, and a treasured recipe that's just never quite the same after they're gone. This is one of those recipes. Juanita Johnston (Nonnie) was a schoolteacher and principal. She was married for sixty-six years to Cecil Ray Johnston, a postal worker, musician, and painter of movie theater signs. Her family always asked for her to bring her special nine-day slaw to every event. It was so popular that when she and Cecil Ray retired and they enrolled in a ceramics class to have something they could enjoy together, the first thing they made was a ceramic cabbage with a bunny on top to hold this treasured recipe. They are both gone now, but this legacy recipe and the ceramic cabbage are treasured by their only son, Billy Joe Johnston, who shared their story and this recipe with me.

3	pounds cabbage, chopped or shredded	1	tablespoon pepper
1	large green bell pepper, chopped	1	tablespoon celery seed
¼	cup chopped red bell pepper	1	cup sugar
¼	cup shredded carrot	1	cup apple cider vinegar
1	medium onion, chopped	½	cup vegetable oil
1	tablespoon salt		

In a large bowl mix the cabbage, bell peppers, carrot, onion, salt, pepper, and celery seed. Stir in the sugar and allow the mixture to stand while the dressing is prepared in a medium saucepan. Bring the vinegar and oil to a boil, pour over the cabbage mixture, and stir well. Make sure all the vegetables are in the dressing. Cover the slaw and refrigerate overnight before serving. This slaw keeps for at least 9 days, hence the name, and according to the Johnston family, it "just keeps getting better 'n' better!"

Makes 14 servings

My sister was always great at treading the dangerous waters of cook-appreciation etiquette. As a young child, she kept asking for more helpings of my grandmother's purple hull peas. When questioned by my mother, she just said, "I don't know, Mama, but I think Grandma's stove just cooks these peas better than yours." She satisfied everyone by blaming it all on the stove. *Now, that's Southern.*

Green Pea Casserole

1	pound fresh or frozen green peas
1	small onion, sliced very thin
2	tablespoons olive oil
1	(4-ounce) jar or can sliced mushrooms
2	large eggs, hard-boiled and sliced
1	(10.5-ounce) can cream of celery soup, heated
½	cup grated sharp Cheddar cheese
1	cup crushed potato chips

Preheat the oven to 350 degrees. In a medium saucepan bring the peas to a boil in just enough water to cover them. Reduce the heat, cover, and simmer for 20 minutes while preparing the rest of the ingredients. In a small skillet sauté the onion in the oil. Drain the excess oil and set aside. Drain the cooked peas. In a 2-quart casserole dish, layer, in order, one-third of the peas, onion, mushrooms, egg slices, cream of celery soup, and grated cheese. Repeat the layering until all ingredients are used. Top with the crushed potato chips. Bake for 30 minutes, or until bubbly.

Makes 8 servings

Yellow Squash Casserole

2	cups sliced yellow squash
4	tablespoons butter
2	tablespoons all-purpose flour
1	cup milk
$\frac{1}{2}$	teaspoon salt
$\frac{1}{2}$	teaspoon pepper
$\frac{1}{8}$	teaspoon nutmeg
2	large eggs, separated
$\frac{2}{3}$	cup seasoned breadcrumbs

Preheat the oven to 400 degrees. In a saucepan cover the squash with water and bring to a boil for 15 minutes. Drain the squash in a colander. Combine the butter, flour, and milk in the saucepan and cook, stirring constantly with a whisk, over medium heat until thickened. Set aside the white sauce to cool. In a large bowl blend the squash, salt, pepper, nutmeg, beaten egg yolks, and breadcrumbs. In another bowl beat the egg whites with a handheld electric mixer until stiff. Fold the beaten egg whites into the cooled white sauce. Pour the squash mixture into a greased 3-quart casserole dish and cover with the sauce mixture. Gently stir the sauce mixture into the squash and bake the casserole for 15 to 20 minutes, or until the top is golden.

Makes 6 servings

Marinated Veggie Salad

3	tablespoons apple cider vinegar
8	tablespoons balsamic vinegar
4	tablespoons olive oil
2	teaspoons minced garlic
1	teaspoon salt
1	teaspoon pepper
1	teaspoon Worcestershire sauce
6	tablespoons sugar
2	medium cucumbers, cut into small chunks (peel left on)
2	large tomatoes, peeled and cut in small chunks
2	medium green peppers, chopped
2	medium onions, chopped
1/8	cup chopped fresh basil

In a medium saucepan, stir together the apple cider and balsamic vinegars, oil, garlic, salt, pepper, Worcestershire sauce, and sugar. Cook over medium heat until the sugar is dissolved. In a large bowl, gently mix the cucumbers, tomatoes, green peppers, onions, and basil. Stir in the dressing. Cover and refrigerate the salad for at least 30 minutes before serving chilled.

Makes 4 to 6 servings

Balsamic Baked Tomatoes

Fresh garden tomatoes can be cut in thick slices and baked with fresh basil, garlic, and balsamic vinegar. Often sweet tomatoes will be left on the stalk in supermarkets, and I bake them with the stalks on and serve them that way. The tomatoes sometime burst open when baking. You can also cut the tomatoes in half and melt a sprinkle of grated Parmesan cheese on top or add cooked bacon bits for another taste enhancement.

4	**small to medium-size sweet tomatoes, halved, thickly sliced, or left whole with stalks on**
1	**cup olive oil**
2	**teaspoons minced garlic**
2	**teaspoons minced fresh basil**
1	**cup balsamic vinegar**
2	**teaspoons pepper**
1	**teaspoon salt**

Preheat the oven to 350 degrees. Place the tomatoes in a 13 x 9-inch baking dish. In a small saucepan combine the oil, garlic, basil, vinegar, pepper, and salt. Bring to a boil. Drizzle over the tomatoes and bake for 30 minutes. Serve hot.

Makes 4 servings

Fresh red ripe tomatoes—washed, peeled, sliced, and served cold and piled high on a plate next to fresh cucumbers— were at every single meal during the harvest season. Tomato gravy, tomato sandwiches, and tomatoes eaten like an apple with a salt shake on every bite— I never knew tomatoes were used for spaghetti sauce until I moved from the South.

Roasted Winter Root Vegetables

During the writing of this book, my friend Pepper Saucier lost her father, Ray. She went home after his funeral and made recipes that reminded her of him. This is the first recipe she made, and she shared it with me. In the South we celebrate with food, we entertain with food, and we grieve with food.

Veggies
4	cups diced raw root vegetables, such as parsnips, rutabagas, carrots, turnips, sweet potatoes, and potatoes
2	tablespoons olive oil
1	teaspoon salt
1	teaspoon pepper
1	teaspoon salt-free seasoning (such as Mrs. Dash)

Drizzle
1	tablespoons maple syrup
2	tablespoons balsamic vinegar
¼	cup chicken broth

To make the veggies, preheat the oven to 400 degrees. Toss the veggies with the oil, salt, pepper, and seasoning. Spread on a shallow baking pan. Bake 40 minutes, or until tender, stirring once or twice.

To make the drizzle, while the veggies are baking, simmer all the drizzle ingredients in a saucepan on medium heat for 5 minutes. Drizzle over the cooked veggies and bake for another 5 minutes. Serve hot.

Makes 4 servings

A BIG SOUTHERN MEAL IN THE SUMMER DOESN'T ALWAYS HAVE TO INCLUDE MEAT. WHEN THE GARDEN IS BOUNTIFUL, GATHERING AROUND A TABLE OF FRESH VEGETABLES, BOTH COOKED AND SERVED RAW, IS PERFECTLY ACCEPTABLE. *Actually, such a meal is welcomed.*

Bacon Baked Beans

1	tablespoon butter
½	cup chopped green bell pepper
½	cup chopped sweet onion
½	teaspoon minced garlic
3	tablespoons maple syrup
2	tablespoons Worcestershire sauce
¼	teaspoon Louisiana hot sauce
¼	cup firmly packed brown sugar
2	teaspoons yellow mustard
¼	cup hickory-smoked barbecue sauce
1	(28-ounce) can pork and beans
6	slices bacon

Preheat the oven to 300 degrees. In a saucepan melt the butter and sauté the bell pepper, onion, and garlic. Stir in the maple syrup, Worcestershire sauce, hot sauce, brown sugar, mustard, and barbecue sauce, continuing to stir over medium heat until fully integrated. In a 3-quart baking dish, blend the beans and the heated sauce. Lay the bacon strips on top of the beans and bake, covered, for 30 minutes. Uncover and continue to bake 30 more minutes.

Makes 10 servings

Granny's Li'l Green Butter Beans

I don't remember a family gathering without butter beans. They are still my favorite. Most people cook them to death, but this way they are garden-fresh perfect with just a hint of bacon. Save any leftover beans for a vegetable soup at the end of the week.

1	slice bacon or 1 tablespoon bacon grease
1	pound fresh baby lima beans, or 1 (16-ounce) package frozen (we call these butter beans)
2	cups water
1	teaspoon sugar
1	teaspoon salt

In a medium-size pot, cook the bacon for about 2 minutes on each side until there is bacon grease in the bottom of the pot (keep the bacon in the pot), or melt 1 tablespoon of bacon grease. Add the lima beans, water, sugar, and salt, and bring the beans to a boil. Reduce the heat, cover the pot, and allow the beans to simmer for about 25 minutes, just until the beans are tender. Stir gently after 15 minutes of simmering to make sure the seasonings are evenly distributed. The juice should be a brothy texture and the beans should be tender but not mealy.

Makes 4 to 6 servings

We picked in the morning, washed in the midday, and shelled into the sunset.

Cornmeal-Crusted Okra

Summer yielded rich harvests, blistering hot days, and the best all-vegetable meals you could imagine. Pan-fried okra was one of my favorites served with fresh sliced tomatoes, little green butter beans, and creamed corn. When I left home and ordered fried okra, I was served these little battered puff balls fried hard around a slimy piece of okra. This was not my kind of okra (pronounced ok-ree where I'm from). So if I was going to get a fresh taste of home, it meant firing up the cast-iron skillet and mealin' up some okree myself!

½   **cup vegetable oil (or bacon grease if you have it)**
1   **cup yellow cornmeal**
1   **tablespoon all-purpose flour**
1   **teaspoon salt**
1   **teaspoon pepper**
4   **cups rinsed fresh okra, sliced in rounds (remove the stems and tips)**

Heat the oil in a large cast-iron skillet on medium-high. Blend the cornmeal, flour, salt, and pepper in a large bowl. Coat the okra with the cornmeal mix, covering each and every piece. If the okra is rinsed, it will be damp and the cornmeal will stick. Pour the okra into the hot oil, and fry, stirring often, until the cornmeal turns golden and the okra is slightly crunchy, about 10 to 15 minutes.

Makes 4 servings

Cajun Fried Green Tomatoes

The fine art of frying in the South can be applied to everything from chicken to Snickers bars. "Never too fast, never too slow, and always in cast iron" will accomplish most varieties of frying nirvana.

½   cup bacon grease (vegetable oil will work, without the hint of flavor, though)
4   large green tomatoes, washed and sliced ¼ inch thick (peel left on)
1½   tablespoons Cajun seasoning
2   cups plain yellow cornmeal (white is fine, too, but yellow is prettier)
⅓   cup self-rising cornmeal

Heat the bacon grease to medium-high (cornmeal should sizzle and bubble when you drop it in to test before the tomatoes are fried). Lay out the tomato slices on a large pan or wax paper. Evenly sprinkle one side and then the other with the Cajun seasoning. Mix the cornmeals in a flat bowl or baking pan, and carefully dredge each tomato slice. Fry until golden on one side, and then turn to fry golden on the other. This will happen fast, about 1 minute on each side. Color is your only indicator. The crust will fall off easily, so carefully lift the tomato slices with a metal turner, and move to a serving plate lined with a paper towel to soak up any excess grease.

Makes 8 to 10 servings

Black-Eyed Pea Patties

2   cups cooked black-eyed peas, drained
1/8   cup chopped green onion
1   (8-ounce) can water chestnuts, drained and chopped
2   teaspoons lemon juice
1/2   teaspoon salt
1/2   teaspoon pepper
1/2   teaspoon cayenne pepper
1/2   tablespoon butter, melted
2   large eggs
2   tablespoons all-purpose flour
1   cup cornmeal
1   cup vegetable oil

In a large bowl mix the black-eyed peas, green onion, water chestnuts, lemon juice, salt, pepper, cayenne pepper, and melted butter. Blend well. In a small bowl beat 1 egg plus the yolk of another, reserving the 1 egg white. Stir into the black-eyed pea mixture and then add the flour. Form the pea mixture into patties, dip in the remaining beaten egg white, and dredge in the cornmeal. Heat the oil in a skillet and fry the pea patties until golden, about 2 minutes on each side. Serve hot either plain or with brown gravy, white gravy, sausage gravy, or ketchup. These are great vegetarian patties.

Makes 4 to 6 patties

Pintos and Sausage

When my friend Ruth Passons left me a phone message saying there were pinto beans and cornbread waiting, I made a beeline to her house! It's simple country comfort at its best.

1	pound dried pinto beans, washed, covered, and soaked overnight in the refrigerator
1	tablespoon olive oil
1	large onion, chopped
2	teaspoons minced garlic
1	pound smoked sausage, sliced
1	green bell pepper, chopped
6	cups water
2	teaspoons salt
1	teaspoon pepper
1/4	teaspoon Tabasco sauce

Pour off the water from the soaking pinto beans. In a Dutch oven or lidded bean pot, heat the oil and sauté the onion, garlic, sausage, and bell pepper. When the onions are clear, stir in the beans and the 6 cups water and bring to a boil. Reduce the heat, cover, and simmer the beans for 45 minutes. Stir in the salt, pepper, and Tabasco sauce and continue to simmer for 15 minutes more, or until the beans are tender. Serve hot by itself, over rice, or with fresh warm cornbread.

Makes 6 servings

Strawberry Sorbet

4   **cups fresh strawberries, pureed**
½   **cup pineapple juice**
¼   **cup sugar**

In a large bowl combine all the ingredients and pour into a 13 x 9-inch glass casserole dish. Cover and freeze until the mix is a slushy consistency. Transfer the mix to a blender or food processor and blend until smooth. Return the slush to the casserole dish, cover, and freeze until it's firm. Scrape out or scoop out and serve in dessert dishes.

Makes 6 servings

An old farmer at the feed store told us that the only thing slugs liked better than strawberries was beer. They liked it so much they'd slide over in the sauce and drown themselves. Since we were Baptist and didn't partake, my mama marched over to Mr. Floyd's one afternoon and asked him for some, since he seemed to drink it by the barrel. He was kind enough to oblige. We cut off the bottom quarters of a bunch of old milk cartons and filled each with the brew. The next morning, we ran out to find all of them filled with slimy, drowned, drunken, dead slugs. *Our strawberry crop was saved.*

Zucchini Cake

2	cups all-purpose flour
2¼	cups sugar
1	cup unsweetened cocoa powder
2	teaspoons baking soda
2	teaspoons baking powder
½	teaspoon salt
1½	teaspoons cinnamon
2	teaspoons vanilla extract
4	large eggs
1	cup vegetable oil
½	cup applesauce
3½	cups grated zucchini
1	cup chopped pecans, divided
1½	cups hot fudge topping

Preheat the oven to 350 degrees. Grease a 10-inch Bundt pan with shortening and then flour, removing any excess. Sift the flour into a large bowl. Add the sugar, cocoa, baking soda, baking powder, salt, cinnamon, and vanilla. Add the eggs, oil, and applesauce, blending well. Gently fold in the zucchini and ¾ cup of the pecans until they are fully integrated into the cake batter. Pour the batter into the prepared Bundt pan and bake for 1 hour. Cool the cake for 10 to 15 minutes in the pan before turning out onto a cake platter.

Heat the hot fudge topping in the microwave for about 30 seconds until fully heated. Stir and drizzle across the entire cake. Top with the remaining ¼ cup pecans. Serve warm, either plain or with a scoop of vanilla ice cream.

Makes 12 to 14 servings

As a child, I always thought the term *pot liquor* was talking about someone who was lucky enough to lick the pot. Until I understood this delicate difference, *I naively did ask to lick the pot a few times.*

Boiled Peanuts, Ribs, and Homemade Ice Cream
Outdoor Summer Celebrations

The front porch is the official gathering place in the South. A swing, big rocking chairs, and a wave for everyone that passes are all part of our DNA. It's where we sip our tea iced and sweet, and our coffee strong and hot, no matter the temperature outside. The Southern celebration of summer is filled with the smells of magnolias, wisteria, and gardenias in full bloom, in harmony with the sounds of crickets singing and cicadas buzzing loudly. The humidity is heavy enough to cut with a knife, and that only adds to the romance of summer in the South. Eating fresh-churned homemade ice cream as it melts down my chin, shelling those right-from-the-garden peas and beans, and watching fireworks over the river are among my favorite memories that inevitably make me instantly homesick. The simplicity of a watermelon on ice, sliced and eaten wholeheartedly "dive in head first" without regard to napkins, my tan bare feet bathed in the overflow, is about as good as it gets.

Baptist Mint Julep

I was raised Southern Baptist. My PawPaw was a Southern Baptist preacher, my father a deacon, and all the women in the family were part of the WMU (Woman's Missionary Union). If you were Baptist, you were taught not to drink, dance, cuss, smoke, or, heaven forbid, fornicate. However, it was hot in the South, and some of even God's front-row best Baptists backslid on a number of those points, especially that last one. But it was perfectly acceptable to fellowship through food and make-believe cocktails. This recipe is certainly toned down from the bourbon, mint, and sugar in the original, but it is refreshing and fun to serve. This is a Johnston family recipe.

Mocktail Syrup

2	cups sugar
2$\frac{1}{2}$	cups water
$\frac{1}{4}$	cup fresh mint leaves
1	(6-ounce) can frozen lemonade concentrate
$\frac{1}{2}$	(6-ounce) can frozen orange juice concentrate

To make the mocktail syrup, boil the sugar and water in a saucepan for 10 minutes. Remove from the heat and add the mint leaves, allowing them to steep until the solution is cool. Remove the mint leaves, squeezing the remainder of the liquid into the solution before disposing of them. Add the lemonade concentrate and orange juice concentrate and blend well. Store in a serving pitcher and refrigerate.

To make the drink, mix 1 cup of the mocktail syrup with 2 cups water and serve over ice in a tall glass.

Makes 8 mocktails

Pineapple Chiller

3   **cups pineapple juice**
¼   **cup lemon juice**
2   **(12-ounce) cans cold ginger ale, divided**
       Pineapple wedges or chunks, for garnish

Combine the pineapple juice and lemon juice and freeze in ice trays. When frozen, dump 1 tray of the juice cubes, one-half tray of regular ice, and 1 can ginger ale in a blender. Blend the ingredients to make a slush and pour into frosted martini or margarita glasses. Repeat this until all the pineapple ice is used. Garnish with pineapple wedges or chunks.

Makes 6 chillers

Extended family is what the South is always about. Relatives know each other. Most even like each other. But even if they don't, they eat with each other.

Corn Fritters

1	large egg yolk, beaten
1	cup fresh whole-kernel sweet corn, cut from the cob
½	cup plus 2 tablespoons all-purpose flour
½	teaspoon salt
½	teaspoon baking powder
1	egg white, beaten stiff
2	cups vegetable oil for frying

In a large bowl combine the beaten egg yolk and the corn. Sift the flour with the salt and baking powder and stir into the corn mixture. Fold in the stiffly beaten egg white. Heat the oil in a large skillet to 375 degrees. Dip the batter by large spoonfuls into the heated oil and fry until the fritters are a medium brown, 3 to 4 minutes. (Do not leave these unattended!) Transfer to a paper towel–lined plate to drain off the excess oil and serve immediately. Always remember to remove the hot oil from the heat when you are finished frying.

Makes 6 servings

The glorious thing about the South is our reverence for the produce our localities are famous for. *There was a festival and a queen for every food.* In the South we salute peanuts, rice, mullet, and just about anything we can celebrate by putting a crown on a pretty girl's head.

Salmon Salad

Chilled tuna salad is wonderful, but a variation on that theme featuring salmon, which has additional omega-3s, is yummy and healthful, especially if you serve it on seedy multigrain bread or on fresh spinach leaves.

1	(5.5-ounce) can boneless, skinless salmon, drained
1/4	cup chopped celery
1/4	cup chopped water chestnuts,
1	small onion, chopped
2	large eggs, hard-boiled and chopped
1/2	cup sliced black olives
1/4	cup chopped sour or dill pickles
1/4	cup sliced almonds
1/2	teaspoon Cajun seasoning
1/2	teaspoon cumin
1/4	teaspoon minced garlic
2	tablespoons mayonnaise
2	teaspoons zesty Italian salad dressing

Combine all the ingredients in a medium bowl. Serve on salad greens or multigrain bread.

Makes 4 servings

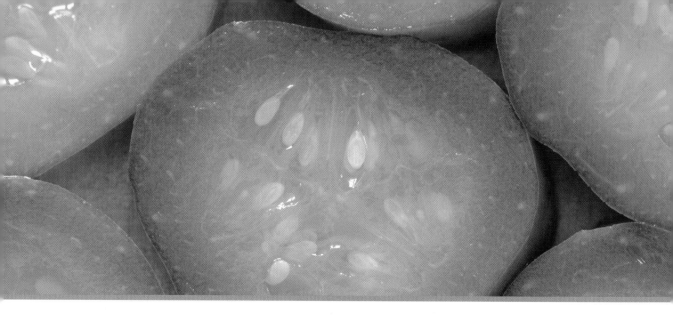

Bread and Butter Pickles

Southern cooking is more of an experience than an exact science. When I asked my mother how many pickles her recipe made, she said, "I don't know . . . a lot of 'em. About a dishpan full." When I asked the size of her dishpan, she said, "Well, you know how big MawMaw's old dishpan was."

Cucumber Preparation
- 5   quarts medium cucumbers, washed and sliced
- 6   medium onions, sliced
- ½   cup salt (not iodized)

Pickle Canning
- 6   cups sugar
- 6   cups white vinegar
- 1½   teaspoons pickling spice
- 1   teaspoon ground turmeric

To prepare the cucumbers, combine the cucumbers, onions, and salt in a large stockpot, making sure the cucumbers are covered with the salt. Cover the pot with a towel and allow the cucumbers to sit for 6 hours. This will pull the water from the cucumbers. Drain any liquid.

To can the pickles, add the sugar, vinegar, pickling spice, and turmeric to the cucumbers in the stockpot and bring the pickles to a simmering boil for about 90 seconds. The pickles will turn a darker green. Put the pickle mixture, with liquid, into 12 hot sterile pint jars, filling to ¼ to ⅛ inch from the top of the jar. Wipe the mouths of the jars and seal with boiled lids. To process the pickles, put the jars on a canning rack in a large canning pot half full of simmering water, making sure the water covers the sealed jars by 1 to 2 inches. Bring the water to a boil, cover, and allow the jars to boil (or "process") in the hot-water bath for 10 minutes. Remove the pot from the heat and cool the jars in the pot for 5 minutes. Remove the jars with a jar remover and store at room temperature for 24 hours on a towel. Check to make sure all seals are good (the lids should be a bit sunken-in at the center). Refrigerate jars intended for immediate use, to chill the pickles. The rest of the jars can be stored, unrefrigerated, in a cabinet or pantry for 2 years, as long as the jars remain unopened and the lids remain sealed. Once opened, refrigerate.

Makes 12 pints

> Porch sitting is not just a hobby.
> *It's an art.*

Boiled Peanuts

Boiled peanuts were my favorite part of summer. I'd sit on the edge of the front porch listening to the crickets sing, and watch the sun go down enjoying our peanut harvest in a divinely salty, earthy explosion. Boiled peanuts were always my reason to stop at Pearl 'n' Sid's in Olla, Louisiana.

Some like their peanuts softer, some firmer, and some folks add Tony Chachere's seasoning and a tablespoon of Tabasco sauce to the water for spicier fare. You can add ice to the water to speed up the cooling process, but I usually don't wait, and dip out the peanuts with a slotted spoon immediately, loving the taste enough to forget the burned fingers!

1½ **cups salt**
5 **pounds green boiling peanuts, washed well**

In a large stockpot, combine the salt with enough water to eventually cover the peanuts by about 3 inches. But don't put the peanuts in yet! Bring the salted water to a boil, making sure the salt dissolves completely. Add the peanuts, cover, and boil for about 45 minutes, or until the peanuts are tender. Remove the pot from the heat and allow the peanuts to cool before eating. The peanuts can be bagged and refrigerated for immediate use, or frozen in bags for later use.

Makes 5 one-pound bags or 10 half-pound bags

Creamy Dill New Potato Casserole

12 to 16	medium new potatoes
1	cup sour cream
1	stick butter, melted
1	teaspoon dried dill
1	teaspoon salt
½	teaspoon pepper
8	slices bacon, cooked and crumbled
2	cups shredded Cheddar cheese

Wash, boil, and cut the new potatoes into bite-size chunks. When the potatoes are soft and cooled, preheat the oven to 350 degrees. In a large bowl, blend the sour cream, butter, dill, salt, and pepper and mix well. Gently fold in the potatoes. When all the potatoes are covered in the cream sauce, pour into a 13 x 9-inch baking dish, cover with a layer of bacon, and top with the cheese. Bake for 20 to 25 minutes, or until thoroughly heated and bubbly.

Makes 6 servings

Special-occasion dinners aren't much different from everyday meals in the South. Eating well is just what we do.

Healthy Harvest Salad

Fresh vegetables and fruits mixed with nuts make a wonderful lunch when it's almost too hot outside to eat. Adding pasta and cheese completes the meal, although this salad is still wonderful without them.

Dressing

¼	cup sugar
1	cup olive oil
¼	cup apple cider vinegar
¼	teaspoon salt

Salad

3	cups cheese tortellini pasta
1	cup mandarin oranges, drained
1	cup peeled, pitted, chunked fresh peaches
1	cup peeled, chunked fresh pears
1	cup sliced fresh strawberries
1	cup chopped walnuts
1	cup chopped pecans
6	cups fresh spinach, washed, drained, tough stems removed
1	cup crumbled Gorgonzola cheese
6	slices bacon, fried and crumbled

To make the dressing, combine all the dressing ingredients in a small saucepan over medium heat, stirring and cooking just until the sugar dissolves. Remove from the heat immediately and allow it to cool completely.

To make the salad, boil the tortellini for about 7 minutes, drain, and set aside. In a large bowl blend the oranges, peaches, pears, strawberries, walnuts, and pecans with the prepared tortellini. Add the spinach leaves and prepared dressing and toss well. Serve the salad on 6 plates and top with the cheese and bacon crumbles, or serve the salad in one large bowl with the cheese and bacon crumbled on top.

Makes 6 servings

Special occasions were special because *everyone came.*

Orange Glaze for Ham or Pork

1   **cup firmly packed brown sugar**
        Grated peel and juice of one 1 large orange
        Grated peel and juice of ½ large lemon
½   **teaspoon cinnamon**

In a medium bowl combine all the ingredients and blend well. Spread thickly on a ham or on pork chops 30 minutes before removing from the oven. To create a brush-on glaze, blend these ingredients with 1 stick butter and use a brush to glaze pork.

Makes glaze for 1 small ham or 4 to 6 pork chops

Marinated Country Pork Ribs

These thick country-style ribs done on an outdoor grill have always gotten me raves. They are so easy, proving that not everything delicious has to be hard.

12	thick-cut country-style pork ribs
1	tablespoon Cajun seasoning
1	(16-ounce) bottle zesty Italian salad dressing
1	(5-ounce) bottle liquid smoke
½	cup steak sauce (such as A.1.)
½	cup Worcestershire sauce

Wash the pork ribs and rub with the Cajun seasoning. In a medium saucepan bring the Italian dressing, liquid smoke, steak sauce, and Worcestershire sauce to a boil. Immediately remove the sauce from the heat. Lay the ribs flat in a baking dish and saturate them with the prepared sauce, reserving ½ cup for brushing while grilling. Cover and refrigerate overnight.

Over medium coals, grill the pork ribs for about 20 minutes per side until done. The inner temperature should be 160 degrees, and the meat should begin to pull away from the bone. Use the reserved sauce to brush on the ribs during cooking.

Makes 6 servings

The best part about peach season was the homemade ice cream. We always had vanilla ice cream throughout the summer, but the fresh peach ice cream was the best. We'd take turns cranking (it took all ten of our extended family members taking a turn to get it just-right frozen). I loved putting the old-fashioned rock salt on my tongue and letting it melt until my eyes squinted. The chunks of fresh peaches and the yellow cream heavy with sugar were so good, and it was the only time all year that we were allowed to make this dessert our meal. *It was so hot in August that it was about the only meal anyone wanted to eat.*

Old-Fashioned Very Vanilla Homemade Ice Cream

This recipe is older than I am. Do not do the math.

1½	**cups sugar**
2	**tablespoons cornstarch**
½	**teaspoon salt**
1	**quart milk**
4	**large eggs**
2	**tablespoons vanilla extract**
4	**cups heavy cream**

In a double boiler over boiling water (to avoid scorching), stir together the sugar, cornstarch, and salt, and then gradually add the milk. Continue to stir until the mixture is slightly thickened, about 10 minutes. Remove the custard from the heat. In a separate large bowl, lightly beat the eggs. Stir a small amount of the custard into the eggs slowly. Blend it completely. Continue adding custard in small amounts, stirring to integrate the custard with the eggs completely after each addition, until all the custard and eggs are blended and creamy. Add the entire mixture back to the double boiler and cook the custard for 5 minutes. Pour the liquid into a storage container, cover, and chill overnight or for at least 6 hours in the refrigerator. Add the vanilla and cream to the ice-cream mixture and blend well. Transfer to a 1-gallon ice-cream maker and freeze according to the manufacturer's instructions.

Makes 1 gallon

Fruity Ice Cream

2   **cups fruit**
2   **cups sugar**
1   **recipe Old-Fashioned Very Vanilla Homemade Ice Cream (page 101),**
      prepared according to directions below

Peel, pit, or remove any green tops from the fruit. Seedy berries like blackberries should be sieved with a food mill to remove the seeds. Cover the prepared fruit with the sugar in a container and refrigerate overnight or for at least 6 hours.

While the fruit is chilling, prepare the ice cream according to the directions on page 101, up to the point where it is chilling in the refrigerator overnight or for at least 6 hours. When both the fruit and the ice cream have chilled, transfer the ice cream mixture to a large bowl and stir in the 2 tablespoons vanilla, 4 cups heavy cream, and prepared fruit, including the juice/syrup. Cover, return to the refrigerator, and chill for 45 more minutes. Transfer to a 1-gallon ice-cream maker and freeze according to the manufacturer's directions. For chocolate ice cream, 1½ cups chocolate syrup can be substituted for the fruit.

Makes 1 gallon

Orange-Cream Ice

3   **(20-ounce) bottles orange soda (not diet)**
2   **(14-ounce) cans sweetened condensed milk**
1   **(20-ounce) can crushed pineapple**

Blend all the ingredients well and freeze in a 1-gallon ice-cream maker according to the manufacturer's instructions.

Makes 1 gallon

Our homemade ice-cream freezer was aqua blue. It was the same color as my Grandpaw's old farm jeep, his aluminum fishing boat, and his truck.

No-Bake Banana Pudding

This is a light, chilled version of the old Southern favorite. It is also my favorite. It's easy and perfect when you are responsible for bringing the dessert to a church function.

1   (5.1-ounce) package instant vanilla pudding mix (French vanilla is wonderful)
1   (16-ounce) container frozen whipped topping, thawed
5   large bananas, sliced
1   (16-ounce) package vanilla wafers

Mix the pudding according to the package instructions. Fold in the whipped topping. In a dessert bowl (clear ones show the layers), create layers in this order: pudding, bananas, and wafers. This should layer three times with the last layer of vanilla wafers, crumbled on top. Cover the pudding and refrigerate overnight before serving. Keep chilled.

Makes 8 servings

I learned back then that in the South, a good cake maker could made a cake that looked like anything she wanted, *from a beauty queen to a prize-winning bass to an armadillo.*

The Easiest Strawberry Cake

Is there a law that you can't use a mix to create "homemade" memories? I think not. Sit and share some good conversation over this cake and I'll wager not one person will point out that you used a mix.

Cake
1	cup sliced frozen or fresh strawberries
¼	cup sugar
1	(3-ounce) box strawberry gelatin
½	cup boiling water
1	(18.5-ounce) box white cake mix
4	large eggs
1	cup vegetable oil

Glaze
1	(4-ounce) package powdered sugar
½	cup crushed or pureed fresh strawberries
1	stick butter, melted

To make the cake, place the strawberry slices in a bowl and add the sugar. Cover and refrigerate overnight. Preheat the oven to 350 degrees. Dissolve the strawberry gelatin in the boiling water and set aside. Prepare a Bundt pan by lightly greasing with shortening and dusting with all-purpose flour or using Baker's Secret floured nonstick baking spray. Pour the cake mix into a large bowl. Add the eggs, one at a time, blending well after each addition. Add the oil, gelatin, and sliced strawberries with liquid. Blend at low speed with a handheld electric mixer. Pour into the prepared Bundt pan. Bake for about 50 minutes while preparing the glaze.

To make the glaze, blend all the glaze ingredients in a saucepan over low heat until well mixed. Pour over the warm cake.

Makes 12 servings

Six of One, Plus One of Another Cobbler

This is perhaps the easiest cobbler in the world. Anyone knows that warm cobbler is great with ice cream on top, but I grew up pouring chilled evaporated milk on top. It's so rich and so good. Warning: If you or someone you love is trying to diet, they will fall off the wagon if you make this.

1	**stick butter**
1	**cup self-rising flour**
1	**cup sugar, divided**
1	**large egg**
1	**cup evaporated milk**
1	**tablespoon vanilla or almond extract (almond is especially good with peach cobbler)**
1	**cup canned fruit, not drained (peaches, cherries, blueberries, or blackberries)**

Preheat the oven to 350 degrees. Melt the butter in a 2- or 3-inch-deep 9-inch square baking dish. In a large bowl stir together the flour, all of the sugar except 1 teaspoon, the egg, milk, and flavoring, blending well. Pour the mixture into the baking dish, over the melted butter. Dump the fruit in the center of the mixture and swirl it around the dish. (Don't blend the fruit in entirely, but leave the "swirls" of fruit.) Sprinkle the reserved teaspoon of sugar on top of the entire mix and bake for 30 minutes, or until the cobbler is golden on top.

Makes 4 to 6 servings

Old-Fashioned Buttermilk Pie

1	stick butter, softened
2	cups sugar
2	rounded tablespoons all-purpose flour
3	large eggs, beaten
1	cup buttermilk
1	teaspoon vanilla extract
1/4	teaspoon nutmeg
1	(9-inch) unbaked piecrust (page 184)

Preheat the oven to 350 degrees. In a large bowl cream the butter and sugar together. Add the flour and eggs, beating well. Stir in the buttermilk, vanilla, and nutmeg and pour the filling into the unbaked piecrust. Bake for 45 to 50 minutes. Cool for at least 10 minutes on a wire rack before serving.

Makes 8 servings

I miss the sound of my grandmother reading out loud from *Progressive Farmer* magazine while I lay on the porch swing, hypnotized by the creak and sway, and savoring the occasional breeze that wafted through.

Louisiana Lemon Icebox Pie

1	cup graham cracker crumbs
$\frac{1}{2}$	cup ground pecans
1	stick butter, melted
1	(14-ounce) can sweetened condensed milk
3	large eggs, separated
$\frac{1}{2}$	cup freshly squeezed lemon juice, with some pulp
$\frac{1}{3}$	cup sugar
$\frac{1}{4}$	teaspoon cream of tartar

Preheat the oven to 400 degrees. Prepare a piecrust by combining the graham cracker crumbs, ground pecans, and melted butter with a fork. Press the moistened crumbs into a 9-inch pie plate. In a glass bowl beat the condensed milk, egg yolks, and lemon juice with a handheld electric mixer until the mixture begins to thicken. Pour the lemon filling into the piecrust. Create the meringue by beating the egg whites in a metal bowl with a whisk until they are foamy. Gradually add the sugar and cream of tartar and beat with a clean handheld electric mixer until the whites are stiff. Cover the pie with the meringue and bake until the meringue is a light golden brown, about 10 minutes.

Makes 8 servings

Honey Boys

This is a very old recipe harnessing honey rather than ginger for a fun cookie that your kids or grandkids will love to help make.

4½	cups cake flour
1	teaspoon baking soda
1	teaspoon salt
2	teaspoons cinnamon
1	cup honey
½	cup sugar
½	cup milk
3	tablespoons shortening, melted
½	teaspoon white vinegar
1	large egg, well beaten

Sift together the flour, baking soda, salt, and cinnamon three times. This fully integrates the flavors of the dry ingredients. In a saucepan combine the honey, sugar, milk, shortening, and vinegar over medium heat, stirring constantly until hot (do not boil). Remove the liquid from the heat and allow it to cool. Blend in the egg and gradually add in the flour mixture, beating after each addition. Move the dough to a large bowl, cover with a cloth, and allow it to rise overnight in a cool place.

Preheat the oven to 425 degrees, turn out the dough on a floured surface, knead well, and roll it out ¼ inch thick. Cut out the cookies with a gingerbread man cutter and bake on a greased baking sheet for 10 minutes. Cool the cookies before decorating, or enjoy them plain with a good cup of coffee.

Makes 3 dozen cookies

FOURTH OF JULY MEANT FIREWORKS!

And the wonderful thing about being raised in farm country was that it was so flat. We could sit on our porch fifteen miles away and watch the town's firework show across the river. You never had to go far to experience fun. The Fourth was fun, but it was just another excuse for us to eat ice-cold watermelon and homemade ice cream.

Easy Mini Fried Jam Pies

1	(12-count) can flaky crescent rolls
6	teaspoons fruit jam
1	cup vegetable oil
2	tablespoons powdered sugar

Lay out the crescent rolls in groups of two triangles. Place a teaspoon of fruit jam in the center of one triangle, cover with a second, and seal the edges with a fork dipped in flour. When all the pies are sealed, heat the oil in a large skillet. Carefully place each mini pie in the hot oil and fry on each side until a light golden brown. Lift the pies from the hot oil carefully with a slotted spoon and place on a paper towel–lined plate. Sift the powdered sugar on top and serve hot.

Makes 6 mini pies

Cherry Icebox Pie

1½   cups graham cracker crumbs
1   stick butter, melted
½   cup sugar, divided
1   (16-ounce) can cherries, drained
    Juice of two medium lemons
1   (14-ounce) can sweetened condensed milk
½   pint heavy cream
1   tablespoon powdered sugar
1   cup chopped pecans

In a medium bowl combine the graham cracker crumbs, butter, and ¼ cup of the sugar to make a crust. Press the ingredients into a 9-inch glass pie plate. In another bowl mix the cherries, lemon juice, and sweetened condensed milk. Add the remaining ¼ cup sugar to the mixture and blend well. In another bowl whip the cream as stiff as possible with a handheld electric mixer and blend in the powdered sugar. Fold the nuts into the whipped cream and stir into the cherry mixture. Pour into the piecrust, cover, and chill the pie overnight before serving.

Makes 8 servings

Iced tea is always served from a pitcher, usually somebody's great-grandmother's pitcher, passed down as an heirloom.

Pimento Cheese, Tea Punch, and Deviled Eggs
What Every Southern Lady Knows

Knowing how to pull together the perfect event with charm and grace is an art that is quite distinctly Southern. Every Southern lass can set a lovely table, make everyone feel welcome, serve delicious food, offer colorful drinks, and look beautiful doing it. Being Southern is being polite, even when your feet hurt and it's 90 degrees with 100 percent humidity. Little details make all the difference in a big event and pull everything together under the familiar guideline of "just love everybody, sugah," even if you don't necessarily.

Fresh Fruit Tea Punch

Girls from the South who pledge sororities are sometimes blessed, as I was, to find a true sisterhood. My Zeta Tau Alpha sisters and I came up with a presentation of "fruit ice cubes" at our Pledge Week's Ice Water Tea that added color and a chill factor, but no difficult fruit you didn't know what to do with in your punch cup. Here fruit ice is applied in a punch bowl.

2	**cups sliced strawberries**
2	**cups sugar**
8	**cups chilled water, divided**
2	**cups strong brewed tea**
1	**cup lemon juice**
2½	**cups fresh orange juice**
2	**cups pineapple juice**
1	**cup peach nectar**
1	**quart chilled ginger ale**

Prepare the strawberry "ice" by freezing the strawberry slices in ice cube trays with water. In a saucepan, melt the sugar over medium heat in 1 cup of the chilled water. When the sugar dissolves, pour the syrup into a punch bowl with the tea, lemon juice, orange juice, pineapple juice, and peach nectar. Stir in the remaining 7 cups chilled water, the strawberry ice cubes, and the chilled ginger ale just before serving.

Makes about 50 servings

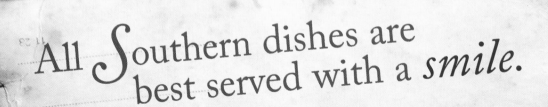
All Southern dishes are best served with a *smile.*

Spring Fling Punch Bowl

1	quart pineapple juice
3/4	cup sugar
1	(6-ounce) can frozen pink lemonade concentrate
2 or 3	drops red food coloring
2¼	cups cold water
1	cup sliced strawberries
½	gallon strawberry ice cream
1	(12-ounce) container frozen strawberry-flavored whipped topping, thawed
1	(1-liter) bottle chilled ginger ale

In a large pitcher or bowl combine the pineapple juice, sugar, lemonade concentrate, red food coloring, and water. Chill overnight.

In a Bundt pan or tube pan, lay the sliced strawberries in the bottom. Then alternate layers of the strawberry ice cream and the strawberry whipped topping to the top of the pan. Cover the pan and freeze overnight. When ready to serve, pour the punch mix in a large punch bowl. Set the ice-cream mold in hot water for 10 to 20 seconds, and then invert the mold and empty it onto a plate. Slide the mold into the punch gently to avoid splashing. Add the chilled ginger ale before serving.

Makes 24 servings

The interesting thing about being Southern and female is the instinct to always be ready to entertain. Whether it's a party in one's own home, a get-together at someone else's home, a charity fund-raiser, or simply an extra mouth to feed at a moment's notice, we are prepared! Throwing together a throw-down from the drinks to the appetizers, finger foods, and desserts is a very important skill in the South. Making things pretty and being gracious to everyone is just part of the plan.

It's simple: Be ready for anything.
Presentation is everything. Treat everybody special!

Nazarene Reception Punch

After an ordination ceremony at Trevecca Community Church, they served the most delicious punch. It's simple and refreshing!

The quantity of this punch can be easily adjusted by keeping a 1 to 1 to 1 ratio of ingredients, and increased right in the punch bowl if you have lots of thirsty guests. It's not a good make-ahead punch because the bubbles are very important to this crisp, cool beverage. It's also a lovely champagne replacement for teetotalers for toasts at weddings.

4   **cups white grape juice**
4   **cups ginger ale**
4   **cups ice, small cubes or crushed**

In a punch bowl combine the grape juice and ginger ale and stir well. Add the ice and stir.

Makes 24 servings

Spinach-Artichoke Dip

Served with fried seasoned French bread rounds or simple table crackers, this party staple is always a hit. Or try serving the dip along with spicy salsa and tortilla chips. For a dip with a kick, use pepper Jack cheese.

1	**(10-ounce) package frozen spinach, thawed and drained**
1	**(14-ounce) can artichoke hearts, drained and chopped**
1	**pound Monterey Jack cheese, finely grated**
1	**cup mayonnaise**
½	**cup sour cream**
½	**cup shredded Parmesan cheese**
¼	**teaspoon salt**
¼	**teaspoon minced garlic**
¼	**teaspoon pepper**

Preheat the oven to 350 degrees. Combine all the ingredients in a large bowl. Spread into a 2½-quart baking dish. Bake for 15 to 20 minutes, or until the dip is hot and bubbly. Serve hot.

Makes 8 servings

Tennessee Caviar

The dish is a perfect vegetarian appetizer, without the bacon, of course! Serve it as a salsa or dip with chips, crackers, or fried seasoned French bread rounds.

³/₄	**cup olive oil**
¼	**cup balsamic vinegar**
½	**cup finely chopped onion**
½	**cup finely chopped green bell pepper**
½	**cup chopped black olives**
½	**cup canned diced tomatoes with green chiles, drained**
1	**teaspoon minced garlic**
½	**teaspoon salt**
¼	**teaspoon Tabasco sauce**
2	**cups cooked black-eyed peas, rinsed and drained**
6	**slices bacon, fried and crumbled (optional)**

In a blender combine the oil, vinegar, onion, bell pepper, olives, tomatoes, garlic, salt, and Tabasco sauce. Place the black-eyed peas in a medium bowl and pour the dressing over the top. Cover and refrigerate overnight. Before serving, gently stir the ingredients together. Add crumbled bacon, if desired.

Makes 6 to 8 servings

Simple,
good comfort
is the signature
of the
Southern chef.

Pepper Jelly

Pepper jelly is a delicacy that I love as a relish with black-eyed peas or crowders, alongside turkey, or with anything that needs a sweet-hot kick.

3/4	**cup chopped and seeded red bell pepper (for color)**
1/4	**cup chopped and seeded hot peppers (jalapeño or any others—you determine your "depth" of kick)**
7	**cups sugar**
1 3/4	**cups apple cider vinegar**
1	**(3-ounce) packet pectin mix, prepared, or 1 (6-ounce) bottle**

In a saucepan bring the peppers, sugar, and vinegar to a boil, stirring constantly. Keep the mixture on a rolling boil, about 10 minutes, until the juice begins to form and thicken. When the syrup is formed, pour the contents through cheesecloth to strain out any solids for a pretty, clear syrup. Add the liquid pectin to the juice, stirring well, and pour into 6 hot sterile half-pint jars, filling to 1/4 inch from the top. Wipe the tops clean and seal with boiled lids. To process the jelly, put the jars on a canning rack in a large canning pot half full of simmering water, making sure the water covers the sealed jars by 1 to 2 inches. Bring the water to a boil, cover, and allow the jars to boil (or "process") in the hot-water bath for 10 minutes. Remove the pot from the heat and cool the jars in the pot for 5 minutes. Remove the jars with a jar remover and store at room temperature for 24 hours on a towel. Check to make sure all seals are good (the lids should be a bit sunken-in at the center). The jars can be stored, unrefrigerated, in a cabinet or pantry for 2 years, as long as the jars remain unopened and the lids remain sealed. Once opened, refrigerate.

Makes 6 half-pints

> *Cooking in the South is like walking.* You do it every day. You do it well. But somehow, when you try to tell someone else how to do it, you leave out a few necessary things.

Stuffed Mushrooms

2	tablespoons butter, divided
½	pound ground sausage
½	cup finely chopped green onions
½	cup finely chopped bell pepper (any color)
1	pound large mushrooms
½	cup seasoned breadcrumbs
1	large egg, beaten
½	teaspoon pepper
3	tablespoons shredded Parmesan cheese
3	tablespoons shredded sharp Cheddar or Monterey Jack cheese

Preheat the oven to 375 degrees. Grease a 2-quart baking dish with 1 tablespoon of the butter. Brown the sausage, green onions, and bell pepper in a skillet until the sausage is done and the vegetables are tender. Remove the mushroom stems and chop them. Set the caps aside. Stir in the chopped mushroom stems and cook for about 2 minutes. Remove the skillet from the heat and allow it to cool. In a large bowl, blend the breadcrumbs, beaten egg, pepper, Parmesan cheese, and Cheddar cheese. Stuff the mushroom caps with the mixture and place them in the prepared baking dish, topping each with a dot of the remaining 1 tablespoon butter. Bake for 20 to 25 minutes until the mushrooms are tender. Serve warm.

Makes 20 to 25 mushroom caps

Pickled Pepper Sauce

Peppers are gorgeous grown in a patio garden, and even prettier when pickled and sealed in lovely bottles and stored in a pantry or kept on the kitchen table. These make great gifts too. Served on greens, cabbage, fried catfish, and even poured in the coleslaw mix, this Southern condiment can be found in almost every eatery below the Mason-Dixon line.

We always saved any pretty bottles, including decanters, salad dressing bottles, and even bath oil bottles, for making pepper sauce. The only key is to make sure the bottles have been washed of any scent or residue, and the bottles are sterile and hot when the hot vinegar is poured into them. Some people add ¼ teaspoon olive oil to the top of the vinegar mix to "bring out the heat" of the peppers.

2	**cups peppers (jalapeño, bouquet, chipotle, cherry, or any peppers with kick)**
3	**cups white vinegar**
2	**cups water**

Wearing rubber gloves (to avoid the pain of pepper on your skin or in your eyes), stuff either clean whole peppers or sliced peppers with the seeds removed into hot sterile bottles or jars. In a small saucepan bring the vinegar and water to a boil, and using a funnel, pour the hot vinegar over the peppers, filling to ½ inch from the top. Seal with sterile new lids. Since this is vinegar and a preservative, the bottles do not have to be processed in a boiling-water bath. The peppers should stand in the vinegar until they change to a darker hue. The bottles can be stored, unrefrigerated, in a cabinet or pantry indefinitely until opened. Once opened, refrigerate. You can actually add more vinegar to the refrigerated pepper sauce as it's used. However, if you do this, the sauce won't be peppery instantly. The sauce will taste like vinegar at first, but the longer the vinegar sits in the peppers, the more it will absorb the taste of the peppers.

Makes about 9 (6-ounce) bottles

Passed-Down Pimento Cheese

Mary Harper Jones is a banker, a member of the Hermitage Rotary, and a true Southern lady. Her friend Suzie would bring this homemade pimento cheese to the office potlucks, and Mary said it was just "rub-in-your-eyes good"! Claiming it was a secret family recipe, Suzie refused to share it until she moved away. She left the recipe for Mary on a Post-it note saying, "Enjoy!" Of course, Suzie withheld a few of her secrets from the recipe, but Mary added a few of her own and graciously shared them with me. The main thing to remember is freshly grated cheese. The prepackaged already-grated cheese is just not the same. Adjustments can be made for taste with salt, pepper, and the amounts of mayonnaise and sour cream. Some people prefer Miracle Whip to mayonnaise. Feel free to be adventurous like Mary and add a little more sour cream.

This pimento cheese is great on yeast rolls for a party sandwich and in grilled cheese sandwiches to add a twist. Personally, I think this recipe is amazing on fresh potato bread. Mary swears that, even though it sounds awful, this pimento cheese in the form of a wreath on a cracker with strawberry jam in the middle is just the best thing ever. It's festive too.

8	ounces sharp Cheddar cheese, freshly grated
8	ounces Monterey Jack cheese, freshly grated
1	tablespoon minced onion
1	(4-ounce) jar pimentos, drained
1/2	teaspoon salt
1/2	teaspoon pepper
1	cup mayonnaise
1	cup sour cream

In a medium bowl blend all the ingredients with a fork until the spread is your preferred consistency.

Makes 4 cups

I still have my grandmother's deviled egg plate. It went to every church dinner on the ground and family reunion for almost eighty years. *I still wash it carefully so I won't wash away her name in her own hand on a yellowed piece of masking tape on the bottom of the plate.*

Simply Divine Deviled Eggs

There are almost as many versions of this Southern delicacy as there are people who enjoy it. No matter what ingredients are used, deviled eggs are usually presented on a legacy egg plate handed down through the generations. This recipe is from my friend Kim McLean, who hails from Greensboro, North Carolina. It is a simple "unencumbered" joy—no pickle, no paprika, just sunny goodness you can't resist.

12	**large eggs**
4	**tablespoons Miracle Whip**
1	**tablespoon prepared yellow mustard**
½	**teaspoon salt**
¼	**teaspoon pepper**

The technique used for boiling the eggs is key. Put the eggs in cold water, bring to a boil, and immediately turn off the heat. Cover and allow the eggs to sit for 15 minutes as the water cools. This cooks the eggs without discoloring the yolks, and leaves the whites nice and smooth. (Boiled eggs shouldn't actually be boiled.) Slice the eggs in half lengthwise and empty the yolks into a small bowl. Blend the egg yolks with the Miracle Whip, mustard, salt, and pepper. Stuff each half shell of egg white with the yellow stuffing.

Makes 2 dozen deviled eggs

Scotch-Irish Eggs

A twist on eggs, this recipe provides a hearty party appetizer for St. Paddy's Day (or any holiday) or a treat for a Sunday brunch.

1	pound ground spicy pork sausage
1	large egg, beaten
3/4	cup seasoned breadcrumbs
3 to 4	cups vegetable oil
8	large eggs, hard-boiled
1/2	cup sweet and spicy mustard

Prepare 8 little sausage "jackets" by dividing the sausage into 8 equal parts and rolling each out into a flat circle with a jar or marble rolling pin. Prepare two dredging bowls, one with the beaten egg and the other with the seasoned breadcrumbs. Begin heating the oil in a large skillet as you peel the shell from each hard-boiled egg, and "suit it up" by enclosing it in sausage, coating it in the beaten egg, and dredging it in the breadcrumbs. When all the eggs are "suited up," place them in the hot oil and fry for 7 to 9 minutes, or until they have a light golden, crunchy exterior. Remove the eggs and drain on a paper towel. Allow them to cool a bit, and cut each in half like a deviled egg. Place the eggs on a deviled egg plate and serve with sweet and spicy mustard in the center as a dip.

Makes 16 pieces

Country Ham Aloha Rolls

6	trimmed small slices country ham
1	tablespoon vegetable oil
1	(8-ounce) container Neufchâtel cheese
¼	cup crushed pineapple, drained
6	dinner-size Hawaiian or potato rolls

In a medium skillet pan-fry the ham slices in the oil on medium heat on both sides for 5 minutes per side. Drain the cooked slices on a paper towel–lined plate. In a small bowl blend the cheese and pineapple to make a spread. Split the rolls, spread the bottoms with the pineapple spread, add a slice of cooked ham to each, cover with the tops, and serve warm.

Makes 6 party sandwiches

Here's what Mama said about our table: Don't ever make a centerpiece that people have to crane their necks to see over. *Always arrange flowers in groups of odd numbers.* Pretty table linens, plates, and glasses just make you feel good, and the food seems to taste better. *Clean as you go, but don't let the food get cold trying to make sure everything is perfect.*

Sausage Pinwheels

I learned how to make these in a high school home economics class as an alternative recipe to cinnamon rolls. They are great for a brunch or a tea party, and even taste good drizzled with maple syrup or topped with finely grated cheese. This is also an easy recipe to change by smearing the dough with savory ingredients like spinach and feta cheese, or sweet options like fruit spread and nuts.

¼	**cup shortening**
2	**cups self-rising flour**
1	**cup buttermilk**
1	**pound ground sausage (any flavor), at room temperature**

Preheat the oven to 350 degrees. In a large bowl cut the shortening into the flour with a pastry cutter until the mixture looks like coarse crumbs. Add the buttermilk and stir the mixture with a fork until just blended. Turn the dough out on a floured surface and knead about 20 times, until the dough is smooth. Roll out the dough into a 14 x 10-inch rectangle and spread with the sausage. Roll up lengthwise and cut the rolls into about ½-inch-thick slices. Place the pinwheels on a baking sheet and bake for about 30 minutes, or until golden brown.

Makes 25 to 30 rounds

MY MOTHER HAS ALWAYS BEEN AN INCREDIBLE COOK, BUT NO ONE REALLY GAVE HER FULL KUDOS UNTIL HER MOTHER PASSED AWAY. IT'S THAT UNSPOKEN RULE OF THE SOUTH. YOU HAVE TO WAIT TO GET YOUR MATRIARCH-OF-THE-KITCHEN STATUS.

Sausage-Cheddar Balls

I have yet to go to a party at any time of year that didn't have these on the finger foods menu. Make and freeze them ahead of time and you'll always be ready for a party or a brunch. This appetizer was one of the first things I learned to make in home economics class.

1   pound ground spicy pork sausage
2   cups shredded sharp Cheddar cheese
2½   cups master mix (page 8) or Bisquick

Preheat the oven to 375 degrees. In a large skillet brown the sausage as you would ground beef and drain. In a large bowl combine the sausage and cheese and blend well. Blend in the master mix with your hands and roll into 1-inch balls. Place the balls on an ungreased baking sheet and bake for 10 to 15 minutes, or until golden brown. These are definitely best if served warm.

Makes 75 balls

Smoked Chicken, Grape, and Walnut Salad

I catered a bridal shower with overnight notice, and this recipe was born. It's chicken salad, but certainly out of the ordinary. Served on buttery croissants or red leaf lettuce, or with a light brothy soup, this salad is pretty and hearty enough to be a meal.

1	tablespoon olive oil
2	cups chunked uncooked chicken breast
1	teaspoon minced garlic
3	tablespoons liquid smoke
1	teaspoon salt
1	teaspoon pepper
½	medium Bermuda onion, chopped fine
½	cup finely chopped celery
1	cup halved green seedless grapes
1	cup chopped walnuts
½	cup Miracle Whip
½	cup sour cream
2	tablespoons spicy coarse-ground mustard

In a skillet heat the oil. Add the chicken, garlic, liquid smoke, salt, and pepper and cook until the chicken is done. Drain the chicken. In a large bowl toss the chicken with the onion, celery, grapes, walnuts, Miracle Whip, sour cream, and mustard until blended. Serve immediately.

Makes 4 to 6 servings

Funerals in the South mean everyone starts cooking.

You don't visit the bereaved wearing red or without a casserole.

It is sad that such manners as waiting until grace is said before eating, waiting until all are finished to leave the table, and using kind comments to thank the hostess have been deemed unnecessary or downright antiquated in today's busy fast-food-furious world. Then, you walk into a Southern home where those courtesies are not only expected but also performed, and you feel all warm inside. You enjoy your dinner instead of being rushed along as if there's something much more important that must be done.

It's not the speed of life that separates the South from the rest of the world, but the speed of respect that we as Southerners have for each other and this way of life we love so much. Respect simply deserves the time it takes to achieve it.

Snowflake Fruit Dip

1	(8-ounce) jar marshmallow crème
1	(8-ounce) package cream cheese, softened
1/4	teaspoon cinnamon
1	teaspoon powdered sugar

In a medium bowl blend all the ingredients. Whip until the spread is creamy. Serve the dip with a fresh fruit plate, including strawberries, pear slices, and melon slices.

Makes 3 1/2 cups

Easy-Freezy Blackberry Jam

3   **cups frozen or fresh blackberries**
3   **cups sugar**
1   **(1.75-ounce) package pectin**
½   **cup water**

Place the blackberries in a large microwave-safe container and microwave on medium for a total of 4 minutes, stirring after 2 minutes. Stir again and let stand for 5 minutes. Stir in the sugar and let stand for 20 minutes. In a separate small microwave-safe container, combine the pectin and water and microwave until boiling, about 2 minutes. Continue boiling for 1 minute. Stir the pectin mixture and add to the fruit mixture, stirring for 3 minutes. Pour the jam into hot sterile jars, seal with boiled lids, and let stand for 1 to 2 hours, or until gelled. Store in the freezer or refrigerator.

Makes 4½ cups

Cherry Divinity

Always make divinity on a sunny day. Humidity wreaks havoc on candy. We were only able to make candy about one day a year in Louisiana. If the divinity doesn't harden or ends up too gooey, do like we do and blame it on the weather.

2½	cups sugar
½	cup light corn syrup
¾	cup water
⅛	teaspoon salt
⅛	teaspoon cream of tartar
2	large egg whites, beaten stiff
½	teaspoon vanilla extract
½	teaspoon almond extract
⅓	cup drained, chopped maraschino or candied cherries
1	cup chopped pecans

In a medium saucepan combine the sugar, corn syrup, water, salt, and cream of tartar. Bring to a boil and cook, covered, until the mixture reaches the soft-ball stage (about 5 minutes after reaching the boiling point). This can be tested in water, but a candy thermometer is easier. Uncover the pot and continue to boil until it reaches the hard-ball stage (about 10 more minutes). Immediately pour into a large bowl with the stiff egg whites, beating constantly. Add the vanilla extract, almond extract, cherries, and nuts, blending well until the candy will hold its shape. Drop the candy by tablespoonfuls onto wax paper and allow to set. When cooled and set, the candy can be moved to a covered container, and refrigerated when not being served.

Makes 16 pieces

No-Bake Fruitcake Bars

I have always hated fruitcake. My grandmother hated fruitcake. Imagine my surprise when she served this recipe as chilled bars on the Christmas sideboard next to the fudge and divinity. It's terrific, even if you hate fruitcake.

1	(16-ounce) box graham crackers, crushed into fine crumbs
2	(8-ounce) jars maraschino cherries, including juice
4	cups chopped pecans or walnuts
2	cups raisins
1	(14-ounce) can sweetened condensed milk

In a large bowl combine all the ingredients. Pack the mixture tightly by hand, forming a rectangular loaf. Wrap in wax paper. Chill until firm and cut into bars. Store the loaf in the refrigerator when not being served.

Makes 2 dozen bars

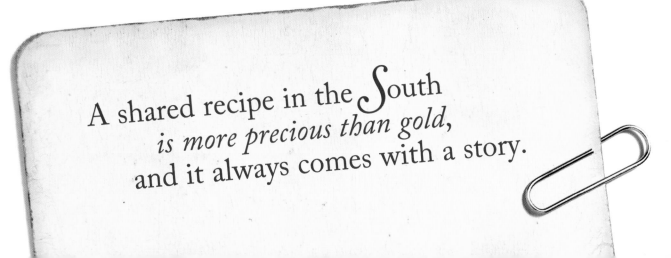

A shared recipe in the South
is more precious than gold,
and it always comes with a story.

Dump Cake

There are about a million ways to make this cake. At a church dinner on the ground, if ten women brought a dump cake, there were ten different dump cakes with different fruits and recipes. This is just one I have always liked.

1	**(21-ounce) can cherry pie filling**
1	**(21-ounce) can crushed pineapple**
1	**cup flaked coconut**
1	**(18.25-ounce) box yellow cake mix**
1	**cup chopped pecans**
1	**stick butter**

Preheat the oven to 350 degrees. Dump the cherry pie filling into a 13 x 9-inch glass baking dish and spread it out to form the first layer. Dump in the pineapple to form the second layer. Sprinkle on the coconut layer. Sift the cake mix over the entire mixture. Sprinkle the nuts as the top layer and dot the entire cake with butter. Bake for 40 to 50 minutes. Serve hot with vanilla ice cream, chilled whipped cream, or thawed frozen whipped topping.

Makes 10 to 12 servings

Aunt Lucille's Christmas Cookies

My friend Pam Holland shared her Aunt Lucille's recipe for cookies. Aunt Lucille was raised in Pulaski, Virginia, with ten brothers and sisters. From the time she married, Lucille loved her life. She cared for her disabled daughter, Faye, who lived into her fifties. Not long after Faye passed away, Lucille left this earth too. Pam told me that most people would see her life and think Lucille had it pretty rough, but those closest to her would say she was always happy, garnering her greatest joy from her faith and her beloved daughter. These are her old-fashioned molasses cookies with crisp edges and chewy centers. Everyone who makes these cookies feels that they've been visited by sweet Aunt Lucille, and the memory of her wonderful laugh and sweet spirit lingers on.

3	**sticks butter**
1	**cup molasses**
2	**cups sugar**
2	**large eggs**
4½	**cups all-purpose flour**
4	**teaspoons baking soda**
2	**teaspoons cinnamon**
1	**teaspoon ground ginger**
1	**teaspoon ground cloves**
	Additional sugar for coating

In the bowl of an electric mixer, or in a large bowl using a very strong spoon, beat the butter, molasses, sugar, and eggs. Add the flour, baking soda, cinnamon, ginger, and cloves and mix well. Cover and refrigerate the dough overnight or for at least 8 hours.

Preheat the oven to 350 degrees. Shape the dough into 1-inch balls and coat in sugar. Bake on an ungreased baking sheet for 8 to 10 minutes.

Makes 7 dozen cookies

Cream Cheese Cupcakes

These are childhood treats with a grown-up flavor. Dress them up with sugared fruits or fruit topping to match the color theme of any party.

2	**(8-ounce) packages cream cheese, softened**
2	**large eggs**
3/4	**cup sugar**
2	**teaspoons vanilla extract**
18	**vanilla wafers**

Preheat the oven to 350 degrees. Line a muffin tin with paper liners. In a medium bowl blend the cream cheese, eggs, sugar, and vanilla until creamy. Put one vanilla wafer in the bottom of each cup of the prepared muffin tin. Pour the cream cheese mixture into the muffin cups, about two-thirds full, allowing room for the muffins to rise. Bake for 15 minutes. Cool the muffins, cover, and refrigerate.

Makes 18 cupcakes

When
someone dies,
bring food.

When someone
is born,
bring food.

When someone
is sick,
bring food.

When someone is
visiting someone
down the street,
take food.

Basically in
the South,
bring food,
take food, and
offer food for
any occasion,
anytime, and
for any reason
and you'll be
doing something
right.

Chicken and Dumplings, Corn Pudding, and Coca-Cola Cake
Cooking for Company

The most important thing to remember about the Southern kitchen is that it's always open. Sharing a meal, a snack, a dessert, or coffee with a friend or family is the best part of living. I've often heard it said in the South, "If you leave my house hungry, it's your own fault." Cooking for people is such a joy for most Southern folks, and no one considers it a chore. We celebrate the bounty of life by sharing it with those we know and those we don't. Door-knockin' Jehovah's Witnesses and young Mormon missionaries got invited in for a meal if they happened by PawPaw's at the right time. Of course, they were well versed in Baptist doctrine from Grandpa's sermon notes by the time they left, along with big smiles and bellies full of some of the best Southern food in the world. I will forever hear his big old voice echoing from the front porch to anyone who drove up, "Ya'll get in here and eat somethin'!"

Bacon Biscuits

When the harvest is yielding those fresh, red, juicy tomatoes, slather some mayonnaise on one of these hot biscuits and add a slice of peeled, chilled tomato from the garden. It's an interesting take on a BLT, and perfect for a snack or a hot day's lunch.

¼   **cup shortening**
2   **cups self-rising flour**
3   **slices bacon, cooked, drained, and crumbled**
1   **cup milk**

Preheat the oven to 450 degrees. In a large bowl cut the shortening and flour together until the mixture resembles cornmeal. Stir in the crumbled bacon. Add the milk and stir briefly until just blended. Turn the dough out onto a floured surface and knead a few times until smooth. Roll out the dough to a ½-inch thickness and cut out the biscuits with a biscuit cutter. Place on a greased baking sheet and bake for 10 to 12 minutes.

Makes about 12 biscuits

Butter Rolls

2   (0.25-ounce) packages active dry yeast
½   cup plus 2 teaspoons sugar, divided
¼   cup lukewarm water
¾   cup lukewarm milk
4   tablespoons butter, softened
1   teaspoon salt
3   large eggs, well beaten
4½   cups all-purpose flour, divided
1   tablespoon vegetable oil
4   tablespoons butter, melted

In a small bowl dissolve the yeast and 2 teaspoons sugar in the lukewarm water. Set aside for 3 minutes. In the bowl of an electric mixer, combine the lukewarm milk, butter, ½ cup sugar, and salt. Add the yeast mixture, eggs, and 1½ cups of the flour. Beat until bubbles form, about 3 minutes. Cover and let rise in a warm place for 30 minutes. Punch down the dough. Using an electric mixer with a dough hook attachment, or by hand on a floured surface, add the remaining 3 cups flour and mix to make a smooth dough. Continue mixing until the dough leaves the sides of the bowl. Brush the top with the oil. Cover and let rise until doubled in bulk. Punch down. At this point the dough may be covered and placed in the refrigerator overnight or until you are ready to make the rolls. Place on a floured surface and knead for 2 or 3 minutes. Roll out the dough to a ½-inch thickness and cut into the desired shape with a 2-inch biscuit cutter. Place on a greased baking sheet or in muffin tins. Brush with the melted butter. Let rise in a warm place until doubled in size. This takes about 2 hours. Preheat the oven to 400 degrees. Bake for 10 to 12 minutes, or until golden brown.

Makes 3 dozen rolls

Old-Timey Rolled-Out Flat Dumplins

In the South, we like our dumplins (not dump-linGs) flat. Flat, thin dumplings that hold their shape are not just great with a good, fat hen with buttery broth. Dumplings can be frozen and dropped in any broth—you can make ham dumplings, turkey dumplings, or duck dumplings—or even in a beefy stew. But here's a quick and easy way to keep your freezer stocked with dumplings for any pot. Dumplings always cook better if they are dried out, and freezing is a great way to do that. Make a lot of these ahead, and keep them in the freezer for quick dumpling dishes anytime. Separate them with wax paper and dredge them again in all-purpose flour before adding them to a dumpling dish to thicken the broth. This recipe is as old as the hills.

½	teaspoon salt		1	large egg
2	cups all-purpose flour		¾	cup milk
2	tablespoons shortening			

In a medium bowl blend the salt, flour, and shortening. In a small bowl beat the egg and milk together, and gradually add to the flour mixture to form a stiff dough. Divide the dough into three equal parts (to make it easier to work with) and roll them out very thin on a heavily floured surface. Make sure you flour the rolling pin as well. With a sharp knife or a pizza cutter, cut the dumplings about 2 inches wide and 2 to 3 inches long. Lay the dumplings out flat on layers of wax paper in a storage container with a lid, and freeze.

When ready to cook the dumplings, always dredge them in all-purpose flour again. Drop the dredged dumplings into a briskly boiling broth and cook for about 10 minutes. The flour will help thicken the broth.

Makes 8 servings

Fresh Cranberry-Mandarin Salad

My Aunt Brenda brought this cranberry recipe to the table some years ago, sans the mandarin oranges. I just love the taste of the two fruits together, so I added the oranges. Waiting until just prior to serving before adding the nuts keeps them crunchy and lets the whipped cream stay fluffy. Honestly, growing up, I hated this salad. It was delicious, but my job was cutting each individual cranberry. It was tedious and maddening. Can you say "food processor"? This device makes the chopping much easier and allows me to actually enjoy the food instead of spending a lifetime cutting little cranberry rounds. This is a perfect holiday salad when the berries are in season.

2	**cups raw cranberries, chopped**
2	**tablespoons lemon juice**
4	**cups miniature marshmallows**
3/4	**cup sugar**
2	**cups mandarin oranges, drained**
2	**cups heavy cream**
1	**cup chopped pecans**

In a medium bowl combine the cranberries, lemon juice, marshmallows, sugar, and mandarin oranges. Cover and chill overnight to allow the flavors to mingle and a syrup to form. About 1 hour before serving, whip the cream as firm as you can and fold it into the salad along with the chopped nuts. Move the salad to a presentation bowl and cover it with plastic wrap. Chill for at least 30 minutes before serving.

Makes 8 to 10 servings

We may not be wealthy, but our food is rich.

Mushroom Gravy

1	cup sliced mushrooms
6	tablespoons butter, divided
3	tablespoons all-purpose flour
1	teaspoon salt
½	teaspoon pepper
2	cups chicken broth
1	cup milk

Sauté the mushrooms in 2 tablespoons of the butter in a saucepan for no more than 2 minutes. Remove from the heat and set aside. In a skillet melt the remaining 4 tablespoons butter, and whisk together the flour, salt, and pepper in the melted butter until blended. Gradually whisk in the chicken broth until completely blended. Whisk in the milk and add the sautéed mushrooms. Cook for no more than 5 minutes. When the gravy is heated through, transfer to a serving container and serve hot.

Makes 4 cups

Watching your weight is *never* something you should do as a dinner guest at the Southern table. *It's rude.*

Comfort 'n' Cream Mac 'n' Cheese

The best comfort food in the world is homemade mac 'n' cheese, and this recipe is extra creamy. With real cream, cheese that melts perfectly, and an ever-so-slight kiss of browning on the top, this recipe will cure what ails you, or at least make you forget for a while.

7	tablespoons butter
3½	tablespoons all-purpose flour
½	teaspoon salt
½	teaspoon pepper
2	cups evaporated milk
2	cups chunked Velveeta cheese
1	(1-pound) package elbow macaroni, cooked al dente
8	ounces mild Cheddar cheese, grated

Preheat the oven to 350 degrees. Melt the butter in a saucepan or double boiler over medium heat. Whisk in the flour, salt, and pepper, stirring quickly to avoid lumps, to create a creamy base. Add in the milk slowly, stirring until creamy. Add the Velveeta cheese and stir well to allow the cheese to melt into the cream sauce. In a 13 x 9-inch glass baking dish, spread the cooked macaroni and pour the cheese sauce evenly over the entire contents. Top with the grated Cheddar cheese and bake for 15 to 20 minutes, or until bubbly.

Makes 6 to 8 servings

Broccoli-Roni Casserole

1   (6.8-ounce) package chicken Rice-a-Roni, cooked
4   cups frozen broccoli pieces, thawed
1   (10.5-ounce) can cream of mushroom soup
½   cup sour cream
½   cup Parmesan cheese
½   teaspoon Cajun seasoning
½   teaspoon minced garlic
6   slices provolone cheese
4   slices American cheese

Preheat the oven to 375 degrees. In 13 x 9-inch baking dish, blend the cooked Rice-a-Roni, the broccoli pieces, mushroom soup, sour cream, Parmesan cheese, Cajun seasoning, and garlic until smooth. Wipe the edges clean and cover the casserole with the provolone and American cheese, alternating between the two. Bake for 20 to 25 minutes, or until golden brown and bubbly.

Makes 8 to 10 servings

As a child, I remember waking and feeling like I would starve to death on days there was a big special-event meal being prepared. The cooking would start at sunup, and I'd wander down to the most glorious smells, but I couldn't have any of the food because "company was coming." It was fend for yourself on those days. Toast did very little to stave off the hunger when there was a roast cooking in the oven.

We always moved the table centerpieces at mealtime because when it came to food, *everything was about having plenty and thanking God for his blessing of nourishment,* and we needed every spare inch of the table to present that bounty. The South is fertile and the growing season is nice and long. So most everything was from the garden, the neighbor's garden, or somebody's garden and we celebrated that with each prayer of grace.

Candied Pumpkin

We always grew our own pumpkins. We decorated with the pretty ones, made lots of pumpkin pies, roasted the seeds, and enjoyed a skillet full of brightly colored beta-carotene with this luscious recipe made from the "not-so-pretty punkins." This recipe will not work with canned pumpkin or pumpkin pie filling—it only works with fresh pumpkin. It is a wonderful companion to any dish with which sweet potatoes would be served.

1	**large fresh pumpkin**
1	**tablespoon bacon grease**
2	**tablespoons butter**
1	**cup sugar**
½	**teaspoon salt**
½	**teaspoon nutmeg**

To prepare the pumpkin, cut in large chunks and remove the seeds. Boil the chunks in a large stockpot until tender. Remove the rind and mash the pumpkin with a potato masher. Measure out 4 cups (save additional pumpkin for another recipe). Heat the bacon grease and butter in a large cast-iron skillet and stir-fry the pumpkin. Gradually add the sugar, stirring constantly. Continue to stir, adding the salt and nutmeg. The pumpkin should caramelize with the butter, sugar, and nutmeg in 15 to 20 minutes.

Makes 6 servings

Cornbread Dressing

On every Southern table, there will be a unique and different cornbread dressing. Some will have giblets (which I cannot stand, so they always go to the dog). Others will have big chunks of chicken. Some will have apples and raisins. I like sausage, so one year I broke the cardinal rule of holiday fare and made my cornbread dressing with sausage. I've done it ever since.

6	cups crumbled cornbread or cornbread crumbs (stale or dry cornbread actually works better)
4	slices white bread or potato bread (without crusts)
4	tablespoons butter
2	cups chopped onions
2	cups chopped green onions
2	cups chopped celery
2	cups chopped green bell peppers
3 to 5	cups chicken broth, divided
2	cups chopped cooked chicken
2	cups sliced smoked sausage or turkey sausage
1	heaping tablespoon dried sage
1	teaspoon dried thyme
2	teaspoons salt
2	teaspoons pepper
1	teaspoon Cajun seasoning
2	large eggs

Preheat the oven to 400 degrees. In a 14 x10-inch or a 4-quart roasting pan, spread out the cornbread crumbs. Dampen the white or potato bread and distribute clumps evenly around the cornbread crumbs. In a skillet melt the butter and sauté the onions, green onions, celery, and bell peppers until the onions are clear. Pour over the breadcrumbs. Stir in 2 cups of the chicken broth. In a separate skillet sauté the chicken and sausage together until the chicken is cooked through and the sausage is lightly browned on each side. Stir the chicken and sausage mixture into the breadcrumb mixture. Add 1 more cup of the chicken broth. Stir in the sage, thyme, salt, pepper, and Cajun seasoning. Stir the eggs into the dressing. The dressing should be soupy. Bake for 20 minutes, remove from the oven, and stir the dressing away from the sides. If you like moist dressing, add another cup or two of the chicken broth, depending on how dry it seems. Stir again and then return the dressing to the oven for another 15 to 20 minutes. The dressing should be firm and lightly, barely crusted on top.

Makes 12 to 14 servings

The nicest thing you can do when you are a guest at a Southern dinner is ask for seconds. You could also ask for the recipe, but I doubt you'll get it.

Plain Jane Peas

Crowders, purple hulls, silver hulls, and all the multitude of fresh peas that turn your thumbs purple and give you hours of Zen shelling time can be easily prepared with this formula. There are a gazillion fancy recipes, but nothing is as earthy and satisfying as field peas prepared well.

2	slices bacon, cut into fourths
1	(16-ounce) package frozen field peas or 1 pound fresh
1½	cups water
1	teaspoon salt

Fry the bacon in the bottom of a 2½-quart saucepan until done. Add the peas, water, and salt and bring to a boil. Reduce the heat, cover, and simmer for 25 minutes, or until the peas are tender. The juice should be brothy. Serve hot.

Makes 4 to 5 servings

Pea-shelling time happened during the summer. We'd all get a pan and begin shelling freshly harvested purple hull peas. We'd shell until our thumbs were all stained a dark purple. It had to wear off—soap, even Clorox, wouldn't remove the color. *Sunday morning during pea-shelling season would have us all in our Sunday best with a pew full of purple thumbs.*

Zesty Zucchini–Cornbread Pie

1	medium onion, finely chopped
1	bell pepper, finely chopped
4	tablespoons butter, divided
6 to 8	small to medium zucchini, peeled and cubed
1½	cups crumbled cornbread
½	teaspoon salt
⅛	teaspoon cayenne pepper
1	cup grated pepper Jack cheese (can substitute Monterey Jack or Mexican mix)
1	cup chicken broth
1	large egg, beaten

Preheat the oven to 350 degrees. Sauté the onion and bell pepper in 2 tablespoons of the butter until the onion is clear. Add the zucchini and sauté until crisp-tender. In a large bowl combine the sautéed vegetables and cornbread crumbs and blend well. Add the salt, cayenne pepper, grated cheese, and chicken broth and pour into an 11 x 9-inch glass baking dish. Stir in the beaten egg. Melt the remaining 2 tablespoons butter and pour on top of the pie. Bake for 30 minutes, or until the pie is set in the middle.

Makes 4 to 6 servings

It's polite to take your plate to the sink when you've finished eating at the Southern table. However,

it's powerfully rude to eat and run.

When you've shared the fellowship of the food, it's important to stay awhile and talk. After all, the cook has spent hours preparing the feast; it's only fair to give him or her at least some of that back in good social banter.

Party Peas

2	(15-ounce) cans Le Sueur peas, drained
1½	cups heavy cream
1½	cups shredded mild Cheddar cheese
1	teaspoon paprika

Preheat the oven to 350 degrees. Pour the peas into a 13 x 9-inch baking dish. Add the cream, top with the cheese, and sprinkle with the paprika. Bake for 20 minutes, or until bubbly.

Makes 8 servings

Garlic-Grits Dinner Casserole

This side dish is a wonderful substitute for potatoes, rice, or pasta. Garnish it with fresh fried bacon bits, ham bits, or parsley flakes for a special presentation. Grits are a staple in the South, and we can always spot visiting Yankees when they try to order just one "grit."

1	cup quick-cooking grits
1	teaspoon salt
1	teaspoon pepper
1	stick butter, divided
1½	cups finely shredded Cheddar or Monterey Jack cheese, divided
½	teaspoon minced garlic
2	large eggs, beaten
¼	cup milk
1	cup seasoned breadcrumbs

Preheat the oven to 325 degrees. Grease a 9-inch square baking dish. Cook the grits according to the package instructions, adding the salt, pepper, half of the butter, half of the cheese, and the garlic. In a small bowl beat the eggs with the milk and add to the grits mixture. Pour the grits into the prepared baking dish and top with the remaining cheese and the breadcrumbs. Dot with the remaining butter. Bake for 45 to 60 minutes, or until the casserole is firm in the middle.

Makes 6 servings

Corn and Sausage 'Puddin'

½	pound ground pork sausage
1	cup chopped red bell peppers
1	(16-ounce) package frozen cream-style corn (canned is fine, but the frozen tastes better)
4	large eggs, well beaten
2	tablespoons all-purpose flour
½	teaspoon salt
⅛	teaspoon sugar
½	teaspoon pepper

Preheat the oven to 350 degrees. Cook the sausage and bell peppers together in a large skillet until the sausage is browned completely. Stir in the corn and when it begins to bubble, add the well-beaten eggs. Stir in the flour, salt, sugar, and pepper. Bake for 25 to 30 minutes in the skillet, until the pudding is set in the middle.

Makes 4 to 6 servings

It isn't the fine china that makes a Southern meal, although many Southern meals are served on fine china.
It's always the love and care that goes into preparing a meal from scratch that makes a Southern table so inviting.

Bacon-Drizzled Wilted Lettuce

Always make this salad after the other food is prepared and everyone is seated at the table. There is a very quick "statute of limitations" on wilted lettuce. It can go from perfection to an overwilted heap in a short while.

1	large bunch red or green leaf lettuce
3	medium green onions, chopped
3	teaspoons white vinegar
½	teaspoon salt
⅛	teaspoon sugar
6	slices bacon

Wash and dry the lettuce, removing the hard "stalky" end. Tear or cut the lettuce into bite-size pieces or strips, as you would for any salad. Place the lettuce in a large bowl and toss in the green onions, vinegar, salt, and sugar, blending the salad well. Fry the bacon until crisp, 6 to 8 minutes, and transfer it to paper towels to drain. While the bacon grease is still hot, pour over the lettuce, toss quickly, and serve immediately while warm. Garnish with the broken bacon pieces. Serve this dish in salad bowls to avoid losing any bacon-vinegar dressing.

Makes 4 to 6 servings

Turkey-Cranberry Monte Cristo

Sometimes an interesting way to reinvent leftovers can become a new "destination" recipe in itself. This recipe will have you roasting a turkey breast and buying cranberry sauce whether or not it's a holiday.

2	cups vegetable oil
4	slices Texas toast bread
2	teaspoons cranberry sauce
6	thin slices roast turkey (a perfect way to use up the leftover Thanksgiving bird)
2	slices Havarti cheese
2	slices honey ham
2	teaspoons honey mustard
3	large eggs
1/4	teaspoon salt
2	tablespoons powdered sugar

Heat the oil in a large skillet. Meanwhile, prepare the first sandwich. Spread 1 slice of bread with cranberry sauce and top it with 3 slices of the turkey, 1 slice of the cheese, and 1 slice of the ham. Spread a second slice of bread with honey mustard and place on top of the sandwich. Repeat this for the second sandwich. Fasten each sandwich together with at least 4 toothpicks. In a large flat bowl beat the eggs with the salt. Submerge and batter each sandwich with the egg. Deep-fry each sandwich in the hot oil for about 2 minutes on each side, or until golden brown. Remove from the oil and place on paper towels to soak up any excess oil. Sprinkle the sandwiches with a fine dusting of powdered sugar, cut the sandwiches in half crosswise, and remove the toothpicks before serving.

Makes 2 sandwiches

Creamy Chicken 'n' Rice

1	tablespoon Cajun seasoning
2	teaspoons garlic powder
1	whole raw fryer, cut in pieces
1	cup uncooked rice
1	(10.5-ounce) can cream of mushroom soup
1	soup can water
1	cup chopped celery
1/4	cup sliced fresh mushrooms
1/2	cup drained and chopped water chestnuts
1/2	cup chopped green onions

Preheat the oven to 350 degrees. Rub the Cajun seasoning and garlic powder over the chicken pieces and set aside. In a large bowl blend the rice, soup, water, celery, mushrooms, water chestnuts, and green onions. Pour the mixture into a 13 x 9-inch baking dish. Nestle the chicken pieces into the sauce and cover the baking dish tightly with aluminum foil. Bake for 1½ hours.

Makes 8 servings

Baked Catfish

This is a great dish served over cheese grits, yellow rice, or wild rice, and served with a steamed vegetable medley.

1	**tablespoon olive oil**
4	**catfish fillets**
1	**large sweet onion, sliced**
1	**red bell pepper, sliced**
1	**green bell pepper, sliced**
1	**teaspoon minced garlic**
½	**teaspoon crushed red pepper**
1	**teaspoon salt**

Preheat the oven to 375 degrees. Grease a 9-inch square baking dish with the oil. Add the fillets. Layer the fish with the onion, bell peppers, garlic, crushed red pepper, and salt. Cover the baking dish with aluminum foil. Bake for 45 minutes, or until the fish is flaky.

Makes 4 servings

You serve the meal with grace.
You say grace over the food.
And you graciously accept the food that's been served.

Stuffed Peppers

I can just think about stuffed peppers brimming with tomatoes, ground beef, onions, and rice and my mouth waters. There really is no "right" way to stuff a pepper. A goulash of leftover veggies can be seasoned and stuffed in a bell pepper and all would be good. Here's a blueprint to get you started.

6	**medium to large bell peppers (evenly shaped and "squatty" ones work better because they stand up)**
½	**pound ground chuck**
½	**pound ground sausage**
1	**medium onion, minced**
1	**teaspoon minced garlic**
½	**teaspoon salt**
1	**(10-ounce) can diced tomatoes with green chiles, drained**
1½	**cups cooked rice**
⅓	**cup grated Parmesan cheese**
1	**cup seasoned breadcrumbs**
4	**tablespoons butter**

Preheat the oven to 375 degrees. Grease a 2-quart baking dish. Cut the tops off the bell peppers and remove the seeds. Blanch the bell peppers in boiling water for 5 minutes and remove from the heat. Place the peppers in the prepared baking dish. In a large skillet brown the chuck and sausage with the onion, garlic, and salt. Pour off any excess grease from the meat mixture and spoon the meat into a large bowl. Blend the meat, tomatoes, rice, and cheese. Spoon this mixture into the bell peppers, top with the breadcrumbs, and add a pat of butter on each. Pour any leftover juice from the stuffing mix into the baking dish. Cover the entire baking dish with aluminum foil and bake for 20 minutes, or until the filling is hot and the peppers are soft.

Makes 6 stuffed peppers

Chicken 'n' Dumplings

If you ask people about their favorite Southern food, the first answer will probably be fried chicken. The second will be the next best thing, chicken and dumplings. There are two things the ladies in our family will tell you are necessary for the best dumpling dishes in the world. First of all, use a young, fat, fresh hen. This gives you the richest flavor. And the second thing my family takes seriously in this dish is the size of the dumpling. The farther south you go, the thinner the dumplings. Farther north, the dumplings are more like biscuits. My family members are thin-dumpling people—hence this recipe.

1	whole young fresh hen (old hens just take longer—ever heard the phrase "tough ol' biddy"?)
1	teaspoon salt
1/2	teaspoon pepper
1	large onion, chopped
2	stalks celery, chopped
20 to 30	frozen dumplings (prepared from Old-Timey Rolled-Out Flat Dumplins recipe on page 14
1/4	cup all-purpose flour
4	tablespoons butter

In a large soup pot cover the hen in water seasoned with the salt and pepper. Stew the chicken, covered, until the meat is tender, 45 to 50 minutes. Add the onion and celery to the stewing water as the chicken cooks. Lay out the frozen dumplings and coat them in the flour. The extra flour will help thicken your broth. When the chicken is tender, remove it from the pot with a slotted spoon. When it is cool enough to handle, remove the skin and bones, and pull or chop the meat into bite-size pieces. Bring the broth to a boil and drop the dumplings in. Add the chicken back to the broth, stir in, reduce the heat, and simmer for 5 to 10 minutes, or until the dumplings are tender. Add the butter for richness. Taste the broth to see if any salt or pepper needs to be added. Serve the chicken and dumplings while hot. We like them served with a ladle of hot Le Sueur peas added to each serving, and fresh hot buttered cornbread on the side.

Makes 4 to 6 servings

You can't bring chicken and dumplings to the family reunion if that's MawMaw's specialty. It would be impolite. You wait until that person dies, and bring your version of the specialty to the wake. *Then it's tribute.*

Onion-Smothered Round Steak

1½   pounds round steak, cut into serving sizes
1   cup buttermilk
½   cup all-purpose flour
1½   teaspoons salt
1   teaspoon pepper
4   tablespoons vegetable oil
1½   cups water
2   medium onions, sliced

Prepare the steak by washing and drying the pieces and pounding with a metal meat hammer on both sides. Place in a bowl, cover with the buttermilk, and soak overnight in the refrigerator.

Discard the buttermilk. In a shallow bowl create a dredge of the flour, salt, and pepper. Heat the oil in a large deep skillet with a lid. Coat each steak well in the dredge and brown on both sides in the hot oil. When browned, remove the steaks and pour the dredging flour into the skillet and brown the flour like a gravy roux. When the flour is browned, stir in the water briskly, blending out the lumps. Return the steak to the skillet, cover with the onion slices, and bring the liquid to a boil. Reduce the heat, cover, and simmer for 20 to 30 minutes, or until the onions and meat are tender. If the gravy appears too thick, just stir in more water.

Makes 4 to 6 servings

My mom let me have a garage sale one summer to make extra money before going back to college. I put lots of my things in the sale, and on a whim, I reached into the cabinet for a couple of those old black skillets that were more than forty years old. Imagine the horror when my mother saw a woman about to pay for them. After a short, and not so minor, altercation, my mother took her long-seasoned black skillets back in the house, and *I realized the value of a seasoned cast-iron piece of cookware, especially when it was old.*

> Wisdom is imparted in the Southern kitchen without anyone realizing it's being shared, or that it's wise.

The Hurried-Hostess Pie

You've got unannounced drop-in guests. You need a dessert quick because, let's face it, you are Southern and you'd be mortified if you didn't offer them something scrumptious with coffee. It's just not how things are done down here. So you have them relax, offer them some coffee, and grab four things from your cupboard as you preheat the oven.

1	**stick butter**
½	**cup sugar**
1	**cup all-purpose flour**
1	**(21-ounce) can fruit pie filling**

Preheat the oven to 350 degrees. Using a pastry cutter, blend the butter, sugar, and flour until the mixture looks like cornmeal. Pour your favorite pie filling into a 9-inch square baking dish and sprinkle the mealy mixture on top. Pop it in the oven for 30 minutes, or until bubbly and golden brown, and serve your good-smelling dessert. Your guests will never believe you weren't expecting them.

Makes 6 to 8 servings

German Chocolate Pie

I love German chocolate anything. This is an old recipe that was folded up in some old things of my grandmother's. It wasn't marked as to where it came from, but it sounded so good I had to try it. Initially, this recipe didn't include a crust, but I thought it would just look better snuggled into a crust than naked in a pie plate. See what you think!

1	(9-inch) unbaked piecrust (page 184)
1	teaspoon powdered sugar
1	stick butter
2	ounces German baking chocolate (half of a 4-ounce bar)
3	large eggs, well beaten
1	cup sugar
3	heaping teaspoons all-purpose flour
2	teaspoons vanilla extract
1	cup chopped pecans or walnuts
2	cups whipped cream
½	cup lightly toasted flaked coconut

Preheat the oven to 350 degrees. Sprinkle the unbaked piecrust with the powdered sugar to avoid a soggy crust. In a small saucepan melt the butter and chocolate over low heat. In the bowl of an electric mixer, beat the eggs, sugar, and flour for 3 minutes at high speed. Add the vanilla, nuts, and chocolate mixture. Pour into the prepared unbaked piecrust. Bake for 25 minutes, cool, top with the whipped cream, and sprinkle with the coconut.

Makes 8 servings

Coca-Cola Cake

When the first lady showed up at Crockett Point Baptist Church with a Coca-Cola cake, you would have thought that she'd invented homemade gold. Everyone had to have the recipe. In years to come, it morphed into 7-Up cake, Dr. Pepper cake, RC and Moon Pie cake, and Sun Drop cake. Basically, once someone introduced making cakes with soda pop, the experimenting and Christian-like competition began.

Cake

2	cups all-purpose flour
2	cups sugar
2	sticks butter
3	tablespoons unsweetened cocoa powder
1	cup cola (*never* use diet soda)
1½	cups marshmallow crème
½	cup buttermilk
2	large eggs, beaten
1	teaspoon baking soda
1	tablespoon vanilla extract

Icing

1½   **sticks butter**

3   **tablespoons unsweetened cocoa powder**

3   **tablespoons cola (again, *never* diet soda)**

1   **teaspoon cinnamon**

1   **cup chopped pecans**

1   **cup flaked coconut**

To make the cake, preheat the oven to 350 degrees. Grease a 13 x 9-inch baking pan. In a large bowl sift together the flour and sugar. In a small saucepan heat the butter, cocoa, and cola just until the mixture boils. Add the marshmallow crème and stir until it's melted into the chocolate. Pour this heated creamy mixture into the flour mixture and blend well. Add the buttermilk, eggs, baking soda, and vanilla and beat by hand for about 1 minute to incorporate air into the batter. Pour the batter into the prepared baking pan and bake for 30 to 40 minutes, or until a toothpick inserted in the middle of the cake comes out clean. This is a cake you frost hot, and it's a leave-in-the-pan, take-to-church-supper kind of cake.

To make the icing, in a medium saucepan combine all the icing ingredients and bring to a boil. Remove the icing from the heat, poke holes over the entire surface of the hot cake with a toothpick, and frost the cake while both cake and icing are still warm. Allow the cake to cool in the pan.

Makes 10 to 12 servings

Coconut Pie

Pie

1	(9-inch) baked piecrust (page 184)
2	teaspoons powdered sugar
3/4	cup sugar
3	tablespoons all-purpose flour
1/8	teaspoon salt
3	cups evaporated milk
4	large egg yolks (use whites in meringue)
1½	cups flaked coconut, divided
2	tablespoons butter
2	teaspoons vanilla extract

Meringue

4	large egg whites
1	teaspoon vanilla extract
½	teaspoon cream of tartar

To make the pie, preheat the oven to 350 degrees. Sprinkle the baked piecrust with the powdered sugar to avoid a soggy crust. In a saucepan combine the sugar, flour, and salt. Gradually stir in the milk. Place the saucepan over medium-high heat and stir until the mixture begins to thicken and bubble. Reduce the heat and simmer for 2 minutes. Remove the custard from the heat. In a small bowl beat the egg yolks. Slowly stir about 1 cup of the hot custard into the egg yolks, beating well, and then add the whole egg mixture into the custard mixture. Bring the custard to a boil while stirring, and once boiling, continue to stir for 2 more minutes. Remove the custard from the heat and stir in 1 cup of the coconut, the butter, and vanilla. Pour the hot pie filling into the prepared baked piecrust.

To make the meringue, in a glass or metal bowl (*not* plastic), beat all the meringue ingredients with a handheld electric mixer for about 5 minutes, until the peaks of the meringue are stiff. Cover the hot pie filling with the meringue. Sprinkle the remaining ½ cup flaked coconut over the top of the meringue. Bake for about 15 minutes, watching carefully so that you can remove the pie as soon as the meringue's peaks are golden.

Makes 8 to 10 servings

Table conversation in the South isn't small talk. The most special of meals always comes with the story of the food's origin. Pay attention. Our Southern history is woven in a quilt made of fried chicken and grits.

Red Velvet Cake, Cobbler, and Pralines
Glorious Southern Desserts

Mile-high meringues, rich puddings, many-layered cakes, creamy candies, chewy bars, and fruity delectables abound in the South. In fact, the only meal that doesn't require a dessert is breakfast, and that's only because the homemade jams, honeys, and jellies are desserts in themselves. The interesting thing about the glorious desserts of the South is they aren't all difficult. Some are incredibly easy, and have been invented out of everything from soda pop to ice-cream sandwiches. There are cakes you dump, cakes you poke, candy that requires a sunny day, and pies that are so rich you almost can't finish a whole piece. But you do, because to leave even a bite wouldn't be polite and would be characteristically un-Southern.

Ol' South Red Velvet Cake

This is an old, old recipe. I read somewhere that red velvet cake was made during the Civil War to bring the husbands back home to their wives. That must have been some cake! I remember that in one of my favorite scenes in the film Steel Magnolias, *the innards of an armadillo cake that adorned the groom's table were red velvet. Basically it's chocolate cake with red food coloring and white icing, but something happens when all the flavors come together that is distinctly Old South. Other places use butter cream or cream cheese icing, but this recipe is old and Southern, and the icing is simply vanilla. You can use organic red food coloring or beet juice for the red color of the cake, but this recipe was from a time when no one worried about things like chemicals, so throw caution to the wind and enjoy.*

Cake

½	cup shortening
1½	cups sugar
2	large eggs, beaten
3	tablespoons unsweetened cocoa powder
2	cups cake flour
¼	teaspoon salt
1	cup buttermilk
2	teaspoons vanilla extract
2	ounces red food coloring
1	tablespoon white vinegar
1	teaspoon baking soda

Icing

1	cup milk
¼	cup all-purpose flour
1	stick butter
1	cup sugar
1	teaspoon vanilla extract

Garnishes

1	cup flaked coconut, lightly toasted or tossed in red food coloring (optional)
10	chocolate-dipped strawberries (optional)
1	square semisweet baking chocolate, grated (optional)

To make the cake, preheat the oven to 350 degrees. Grease and flour two 9-inch round cake pans or line with parchment paper. In a large bowl cream the shortening, sugar, and eggs. In a separate bowl sift together the cocoa, flour, and salt three times to make sure that the flavors are integrated totally. (Dry ingredients are hard to blend well with a spoon.) Add this dry mix to the creamed mixture, alternately with the buttermilk, constantly blending. Then fold in the vanilla and blend in the red food coloring until the batter is, well, red. Add the vinegar and baking soda, blend, and pour into the prepared pans. Bake for 25 to 30 minutes, or until a toothpick inserted in the middle of the cake comes out clean. Cool on wire racks while preparing the icing.

To make the icing, cook the milk and flour in a saucepan, stirring constantly over medium heat until the mixture has the texture of pudding. Remove from the heat and cool. While the milk mixture cools, in a medium bowl cream the butter, sugar, and vanilla. Add to the cooled flour mixture and whip by hand or with a handheld electric mixer until the mixture is creamy and has the consistency of icing.

Turn one layer of the cake out on a cake plate and ice the top of the cake. Place the second layer of the cake on the frosted layer and ice the top. (If you would like to ice the sides of the cake, simply double the icing recipe.) If desired, sprinkle toasted or colored coconut flakes on top for garnish. Another pretty garnish is to place chocolate-dipped strawberries on top, placing the larger end of the strawberries down and letting the cones stick up. Similar-size berries placed around the outer edge of the cake top are just so pretty! Another finishing touch is a light dusting with semisweet chocolate.

Makes 12 to 14 servings

The cake plate *always* had a cake.
The pie plate *always* had a pie.
The cookie jar *always* had cookies.

Milky Way Cake

There is no end to what a sweet little Southern church lady will dream up to bring to a dinner on the ground when she's trying to be original. Candy bars have long been a source of inspiration. The basic rule of thumb for coming up with a dessert recipe like this is that if a candy bar tastes good by itself, try making a cake with it!

Cake
8	Milky Way candy bars (Snickers bars also work)
3	sticks butter, divided
2	cups sugar
4	large eggs, beaten
1¼	cups buttermilk
2½	cups cake flour
½	teaspoon baking soda
2	teaspoons vanilla extract
1	cup chopped pecans

Icing

1½	**cups sugar**
1	**stick butter**
1	**(5-ounce) can evaporated milk**
1	**cup marshmallow crème**
1	**(6-ounce) package semisweet chocolate chips**

Garnishes

¼	**cup chopped pecans**
¼	**cup caramel ice-cream topping, melted**

To make the cake, preheat the oven to 375 degrees. Grease and flour an 11 x 7-inch baking pan. In a saucepan melt the Milky Way bars and 1 stick of the butter and set aside to cool. In a large bowl cream the sugar and the remaining 2 sticks butter. Add the beaten eggs to the creamed mixture and continue to beat until fluffy. Add the buttermilk to the creamed mixture and blend well. Add the flour, baking soda, and vanilla, blending until completely integrated. Fold the candy bar mixture into the batter and then fold in the nuts. Pour into the prepared baking pan and bake for 50 to 60 minutes, or until a toothpick inserted in the middle of the cake comes out clean.

To make the icing, while the cake is baking, cook the sugar, butter, and evaporated milk in a large saucepan over medium-low heat until the mixture reaches the soft-ball stage (this can easily be determined with a candy thermometer). Remove the icing from the heat and add the marshmallow crème and chocolate chips, stirring until blended.

When the cake is finished baking, punch holes across the surface of the entire cake in the pan. Ice the cake in the pan and sprinkle the top with the chopped nuts and drizzle with the hot caramel topping. Allow the cake to cool in the pan before serving.

Makes 12 servings

Buttermilk Pralines

2   cups sugar
1   cup buttermilk
1   teaspoon baking soda
1   teaspoon vanilla extract
1   cup chopped pecans

In a saucepan bring the sugar, buttermilk, baking soda, and vanilla to a boil and continue to boil until the mixture reaches the soft-ball stage (this can easily be determined with a candy thermometer). Immediately remove the syrup from the heat and beat until the mixture is thick and creamy. Fold in the pecans and drop into patty-shaped splatters onto wax paper. Use a tablespoon for smaller pralines or a large serving spoon for larger pralines. When the pralines are cool, they can be served or stored in a covered container at room temperature.

Makes 16 to 20 pralines

Southern ladies will offer you a dessert that will send you into a whirlwind of joy. When you compliment them, they will say, *"Oh, it was easy! Just a little of this or that . . ."* In truth, they probably spent half the day working on the perfect dessert to get that perfect reaction. They'll smile with an "aw shucks" attitude; while inside they are filled with delight that you loved their culinary offering. We accept our compliments humbly in the South, but inside we are immeasurably proud of our food.

Berry Cobbler

There is a collection of pretty, yet worn, recipe cards in my mother's handwriting. Some are splattered with years of cooking with love. Somewhere on the card it will say "A Pat Ford Original." This is one of the very best!

Pastry

2	cups master mix (page 8) or Bisquick
1	stick butter
1/4	cup water

Filling

4	cups berries (blackberries, huckleberries, dewberries, blueberries, or any fresh berry)
1 1/2	cups sugar
1	cup water
1/4	cup sugar for sprinkling
4	tablespoons butter for dotting

To make the pastry, blend the master mix and butter with a pastry cutter until the mixture is the consistency of cornmeal. Set aside 1/3 cup of this mixture. Add the water to the remaining mixture and blend. Roll out on a floured surface to 1/2 inch and cut in 1-inch-wide strips.

To make the filling, heat the berries, sugar, and water in a saucepan over medium heat just until the sugar dissolves. Preheat the oven to 350 degrees. Pour the berries into a 13 x 9-inch baking dish. Sprinkle the reserved 1/3 cup pastry mixture over the filling and stir in. Lattice the top with the pastry strips. Sprinkle with the sugar and dot with the butter. Bake for 35 to 45 minutes, or until the crust is golden brown. Allow to cool for at least 10 minutes before serving. Serve with vanilla ice cream or with chilled evaporated milk drizzled on top.

Makes 10 to 12 servings

Easy as Piecrust

A good tip for making a pie with a fresh piecrust and a custard-based filling is to sprinkle the crust basin with one teaspoon of powdered sugar before pouring in the pie filling. It keeps the crust from getting soggy.

3	cups all-purpose flour
1	teaspoon salt
1¼	cups butter-flavored shortening
1	large egg
4	tablespoons water
1	teaspoon white vinegar

In a large bowl work together the flour, salt, and shortening with a fork or pastry cutter. In a small bowl beat the egg well and then gradually add the water and vinegar, blending as you go. Add the egg mixture to the flour mixture. Divide the dough into 3 equal parts. Roll out on a floured surface to use, or wrap in plastic wrap and store in a covered container in the refrigerator or freezer for later use.

When ready to use, thaw the dough if frozen and roll each piece out on a floured surface to a 12-inch circle, ⅛ inch thick. Gently lift each crust and place over a 9-inch pie plate. (For deep-dish piecrusts, divide the dough into 2 pieces and roll each out to a 13-inch circle, ⅛ inch thick. Place each over a deep-dish pie plate.) Lightly press the crust into the bottom of the pie plate and to the sides, and use a knife or kitchen scissors to cut the excess from around the edges. Flute the edges by pressing the dough together in ¼-inch sections between the thumb and index finger, all around the edge of the pie plate. Prick the bottom of the crust with a fork.

To bake an empty piecrust, preheat the oven to 425 degrees. Cover the crust with a smaller aluminum pie plate or pie weights to prevent it from puffing in the middle. Bake for 12 to 15 minutes, until lightly golden. Cool the crust before filling.

Makes 3 nine-inch piecrusts or 2 deep-dish piecrusts (or pastry strips for cobblers, pot pies, or fried pies)

Candies, cakes, pies, and puddings are the punctuation at the end of every Southern culinary sentence.

Fig Preserves

We had fig trees. Other than being the home to a million birds (not a place to walk under in the afternoon), they were the source of tons of biblical fruit that became some of our favorite preserves during the year and the moist, gooey flavoring for the yummy Bundt cake on the next page.

6	**quarts fresh figs, with stems removed with a knife**
½	**cup baking soda**
6	**pounds sugar**
1	**lemon, sliced thin**

To clean the figs, place them in a large stockpot and pour the baking soda over them. Cover the figs with cold water and allow them to soak for 30 minutes in the soda water. Drain the figs and rinse with more cold water. Return the wet rinsed figs to the stockpot and cover with the sugar. Cover the pot and allow the figs to sit overnight as the sugar melts and forms syrup. Add the lemon slices to the figs. Transfer the mixture to the stovetop and simmer over low heat very slowly so as not to scorch the figs. Press down on the figs, but do not stir them. When they begin to bubble, press down on the figs gently with a large spoon. Cook over low heat for about 6 hours, or until the syrup thickens and coats the spoon. While still hot and bubbling, spoon the figs into 5 hot sterile pint jars, filling to within ¼ inch from the top. Wipe the tops of the jars clean and seal with boiled lids. The jars can be stored, unrefrigerated, in a cabinet or pantry for 2 years, as long as the jars remain unopened and the lids remain sealed. Once opened, refrigerate.

Make about 5 pints

Fig Cake

Cake

1½	cups sugar
3	large eggs
¾	cup vegetable oil
2½	cups all-purpose flour
1	teaspoon baking soda
½	teaspoon ground cloves
½	teaspoon cinnamon
½	teaspoon allspice
⅛	teaspoon salt
½	cup buttermilk
1	teaspoon vanilla extract
1	cup fig preserves (page 186), chopped, with stems removed
1	cup chopped pecans or walnuts

Glaze

1	stick butter
1	cup sugar
1	teaspoon all-purpose flour
½	cup buttermilk
½	teaspoon baking soda
1	teaspoon vanilla extract

To make the cake, preheat the oven to 325 degrees. Grease and flour a Bundt pan. In a large bowl blend the sugar and eggs. Add the oil. In a separate bowl sift together the flour, baking soda, cloves, cinnamon, allspice, and salt. Alternately add the flour mixture and the buttermilk to the egg mixture. Stir in the vanilla, fig preserves, and nuts, gently blending. Pour into the prepared pan and bake for 1 to 1½ hours, or until done.

To make the glaze, melt the butter in a saucepan. Stir in the sugar and flour and blend until smooth. In a small bowl beat together the buttermilk, baking soda, and vanilla and blend into the butter mixture. Cook for 3 minutes. Turn out the cake and glaze while it's still warm.

Makes 12 to 14 servings

Mama's Limelight Cheesecake Pie

Can you make a rich dessert with light ingredients that tastes better than it should? Of course you can, if you are Southern! My mother also tried this recipe with freshly squeezed orange juice and said it was a "delicately flavored orange whip of a pie." If you try the orange version, add ½ teaspoon orange flavoring as well.

2   (8-ounce) packages fat-free cream cheese
3   large eggs, separated
1   (14-ounce) can fat-free sweetened condensed milk
½   cup lime juice
6   tablespoons sugar
1   (9-inch) baked piecrust (page 184) or graham cracker crust

Preheat the oven to 325 degrees. In the bowl of an electric mixer, blend the cream cheese and egg yolks until they are creamy. Add the condensed milk and whip until fluffy. Add the lime juice and whip. In a separate glass bowl beat the egg whites with a handheld electric mixer until they begin to get stiff, and then gradually add the sugar, continuing to beat the mixture as if you were making meringue. When the sweetened egg whites begin to make stiff peaks, fold them into the lime mixture. Pour the filling into the piecrust. The crust will be very full. Bake the pie for 30 minutes. Let the pie cool for 10 to 15 minutes, and then refrigerate it in a covered pie keeper (or covered with plastic wrap held up by toothpicks) until chilled, at least 30 minutes, before serving. If you don't allow the pie to cool before you chill it, it will sweat or "weep," creating a less attractive presentation.

Makes 8 to 10 servings

Peanut Butter Bars

Everything is better with peanut butter. I swear, I could lick it right from the jar. Okay, I have, but using it in this recipe is more polite. This is one of my mother's original dessert creations.

1	stick butter
1	cup firmly packed brown sugar
1	cup granulated sugar
1/8	teaspoon salt
1	tablespoon vanilla extract
3	large eggs
4	heaping tablespoons crunchy peanut butter
1/3	cup all-purpose flour

Preheat the oven to 325 degrees. Grease and flour a 16 x 11 x 1-inch sheet pan. Melt the butter in a small saucepan. In a large bowl combine the butter, sugars, salt, and vanilla, blending well. Add the eggs to the mixture, one at a time, blending well after each addition. Stir in the peanut butter. Blend in the flour last and stir until just blended. Pour the batter into the prepared pan and bake for 30 minutes. Cool, cut into bars, and store in an airtight container when not being served. For a delicious treat, reheat a bar for 10 seconds in the microwave and serve drizzled with hot fudge and vanilla ice cream.

Makes 2 dozen bars

Snowball Coconut Cake

Marilyn Allen, a true Georgia peach, sends me recipes that are tried-and-true and absolutely delicious. When I asked to include this cake recipe in my cookbook, she politely told me that the real credit belongs to Linda Jane Allen Tatham from Knoxville, Tennessee. She made it for all the Allen family special occasions. And when Linda Jane was asked about using the recipe, she said, of course. But she had gotten it twenty-five years ago from a girl who used to work at Chapman Drug. So in true Southern tradition, this recipe has circulated from a friend of a friend of a friend, and like good ol' Southern gossip, a little something changes with every new rendition.

1   (18.25-ounce) package French vanilla cake mix

Filling
1   (16-ounce) container sour cream
1   cup sugar
1   cup frozen grated coconut

Topping
1   (16-ounce) container frozen whipped topping, thawed
1   cup frozen grated coconut

Bake the cake as directed in two 8-inch round cake pans lined with parchment paper. Cool on wire racks and cut the cakes in half horizontally, creating 4 layers.

To make the filling, combine the sour cream, sugar, and frozen coconut in a bowl. Ice the top and sides of the first cake layer with one-third of the filling. When the second layer is in place, ice the top and sides with one-third of the filling. When the third layer is in place, ice the top and sides with the remaining one-third of the filling. Top with the fourth cake layer.

For the topping, spread the whipped topping on the top layer, shaping the topping so that the top of the cake looks rounded. Pat the coconut in place with your hands until the cake resembles a big snowball. Serve the cake immediately or store it in a covered cake keeper in the refrigerator until you are ready to serve it. This cake is so refreshing, it is like a snowball on a hot day.

Makes 12 to 14 servings

Blonde Brownies

2	cups firmly packed brown sugar
2	large eggs, beaten
2	teaspoons vanilla extract
1½	sticks butter, melted
2	cups all-purpose flour
1	teaspoon salt
2	teaspoons baking powder
1	teaspoon baking soda
½	cup chopped pecans or walnuts
1	cup semisweet chocolate chips

Preheat the oven to 350 degrees. Grease and flour a 13 x 9-inch baking pan. In a large bowl blend the sugar, beaten eggs, and vanilla into the butter. In another bowl, sift together the flour, salt, baking powder, and baking soda. Gradually mix the flour mixture, a little at a time, into the butter mixture. Fold in the nuts. Pour the batter into the prepared baking pan. Sprinkle the chocolate chips on top of the batter and bake the brownies for 30 minutes. When cool, cut into squares.

Makes about 2 dozen brownies

I can still remember licking the spoon from the bowl my grandmother made her coconut pie filling in. It was a heavy metal mixing bowl, dulled from years of stirring. I must admit that the only reason any residue from that coconut pie ever remained in the bowl was because none of us could fit our heads in the bowl to lick it clean.

Strawberry Coconut Cream Pie

This incredibly easy pie is creamy and delicious, but not nearly as decadent as it tastes!

1   (12-ounce) container frozen whipped topping, thawed
½   cup sliced fresh strawberries
½   cup flaked coconut
¼   teaspoon vanilla extract
1   (6-ounce) container strawberry yogurt
1   (9-inch) graham cracker piecrust

In a large bowl blend the whipped topping, strawberries, coconut, vanilla, and yogurt. Pour into the graham cracker piecrust. Chill the pie before serving. This is also yummy drizzled with a bit of chocolate syrup.

Makes 8 to 10 servings

Piecrusts were in a constant state
of trial and error in our house,
from vinegar crusts to oil crusts to
cookie-crumb crusts of all kinds.
Just to be on the safe side, we
always kept frozen store-bought
crusts ready at all times
*just in case we needed to
break out in spontaneous pies.*

Apple Crumble Pie

This is a wonderful fresh apple-tasting pie. It can also be made without cinnamon for those who don't like that spice.

Pie

½	teaspoon cinnamon
¼	teaspoon salt
½	cup firmly packed dark brown sugar
½	cup granulated sugar
1	(9-inch) unbaked piecrust (page 184)
4	cups peeled and sliced apples
1	stick butter

Crumble

1	cup all-purpose flour
1	stick butter
½	cup firmly packed brown sugar
¼	teaspoon salt

To make the pie, preheat the oven to 350 degrees. Sift together the cinnamon, salt, and sugars in a large bowl. In the piecrust, layer the apple slices and sprinkle each layer with the sugar mixture and a few dots of butter.

To make the crumble, cut together all the crumble ingredients in a small bowl. Cover the top of the pie with the crumble topping and bake the pie for 1 hour. For crisper apples, bake for about 45 minutes. Cool the pie for about 15 minutes and serve warm, topped with vanilla ice cream.

Makes 8 to 10 servings

Orange Cake

Cake

1	cup shortening
2	cups sugar
1	tablespoon grated orange rind
1/8	teaspoon salt
4	large eggs
2	teaspoons baking soda
1½	cups buttermilk
1	tablespoon orange juice
1	cup mandarin orange slices, drained and pureed
2	cups chopped pecans
4	cups all-purpose flour

Glaze

2	cups powdered sugar
1	cup orange juice

To make the cake, preheat the oven to 350 degrees. Grease a 9 x 5-inch loaf pan. In a large bowl cream together the shortening, sugar, orange rind, and salt. Add the eggs, one at a time, beating well after each addition. In a small bowl dissolve the baking soda in the buttermilk and add this to the cake batter. Beat well and fold in the orange juice, orange puree, and pecans. Stir in the flour and blend well. Pour into the prepared pan and bake for 1 hour. Cool on a wire rack for 10 minutes and turn out on a plate before glazing.

To make the glaze, combine the glaze ingredients in a bowl. Use a toothpick to make holes across the top of the loaf and spread the glaze on the cooled cake while the glaze is still warm.

Makes 10 to 12 servings

Easy Apricot Nectar Poke Cake

The glaze is absorbed into this cake for a tantalizingly moist dessert, perfect for any event.

Cake

1	**(18.25-ounce) box yellow cake mix**
1	**(3.4-ounce) package lemon or peach gelatin**
1/8	**teaspoon salt**
3/4	**cup vegetable oil**
3/4	**cup apricot nectar**
4	**large eggs**

Glaze

3/4	**cup apricot nectar**
1/4	**cup lemon juice**
2	**cups powdered sugar**

To make the cake, preheat the oven to 325 degrees. Grease and flour a Bundt or tube pan. Shake out any excess flour. In the bowl of an electric mixer, mix the cake mix and gelatin. Add the salt, oil, and apricot nectar and blend for 2 to 3 minutes. Add the eggs, one at a time, beating well after each addition. Pour the batter into the prepared pan and bake for 1 hour.

To make the glaze, combine all the glaze ingredients in a bowl. When the cake is done and still hot, poke the entire top of the cake full of holes with a toothpick. Pour the glaze over the cake when it's still hot in the pan. Allow the cake to cool entirely. Turn out the cake and keep it in a covered cake keeper.

Makes 14 to 16 servings

If you bake fresh desserts,
the house will smell so good,
no one will notice if things
get a little cluttered.

Ribbon Cane Popcorn Balls

I will always remember spending the first week of deer season in our family deer camp. It was a week of no running water and no fancy stoves. There were Dutch ovens, a woodstove, and fires. But the meals were some of the most wonderful I've ever had. I will never forget knocking on the door of my Aunt Maggie Walker's camper, and there she was in the middle of nowhere with no comforts of a home kitchen, making homemade popcorn balls. My grandmother's popcorn balls were small, the size of her hands, about the size of a tennis ball. This recipe is one I created using my favorite syrup, Steen's ribbon cane dark syrup.

1	cup sugar
1/3	cup ribbon cane dark syrup
1/3	cup water
4	tablespoons butter
1/2	teaspoon salt
1	teaspoon apple cider vinegar
2	teaspoons vanilla extract
3	quarts popped corn (remove any unpopped kernels)

Before you start this recipe, purchase a candy thermometer. It makes the difference in making all candies. In a large saucepan combine the sugar, syrup, water, butter, salt, and vinegar and cook over medium heat, stirring until all the sugar is dissolved. Reduce the heat and continue to stir the mixture until the syrup reaches 270 degrees on the candy thermometer or the brittle-ball stage when you drop some in cold water. Remove the mixture from the heat and stir in the vanilla. In a large bowl pour the syrup over the popped corn and stir until all the kernels are coated. Butter your hands and shape the sticky popcorn into small balls, about the size of a tennis ball. This size is much easier to eat. The balls can be wrapped individually and tied with cute bows and given as gifts. Store the popcorn balls in a closed container.

Makes 14 to 16 balls

There was never a store-bought cake or pie in our house, my entire life. We bought vanilla wafers and Oreos, but they were for making desserts. My first taste of a store-bought cake was at a friend's birthday party, and I couldn't wait to experience those beautiful roses and decorated cakes that all the other kids got to have, while I only got homemade ones. One bite, and I realized that judging a book by its cover was definitely the wrong way to go about a dessert. I have counted my homemade blessings ever since!

Fresh Strawberry Pie

2   **(16-ounce) cartons fresh strawberries, with tops removed, divided**
3½   **tablespoons cornstarch**
1   **cup sugar**
2   **teaspoons lemon juice**
1   **(9-inch) baked piecrust (page 184)**
1   **(12-ounce) container frozen whipped topping, thawed**

Crush 1 cup of the berries in a small bowl. In a saucepan combine the crushed berries, cornstarch, sugar, and lemon juice and cook over medium heat, stirring constantly, until the mixture thickens. Remove the mixture from the heat and allow it to cool. Meanwhile, slice the remaining fresh berries and arrange them in the baked piecrust. Pour the cooled berry mixture over the fresh berries and top with the whipped topping. Put the pie in a covered pie keeper (or cover with plastic wrap held up by toothpicks) and chill until you are ready to serve the pie.

Makes 8 to 10 servings

Peanut Butter Cup Pie

Piecrust

1	(16-ounce) box chocolate or vanilla wafers
¼	cup ground honey-roasted peanuts
1	stick butter, melted

Filling

1	(8-ounce) package cream cheese, softened
¾	cup honey
3	tablespoons smooth or crunchy peanut butter
1	(8-ounce) container frozen whipped topping, thawed
	Hot fudge ice-cream topping for garnish

To make the piecrust, grind the wafers and peanuts together and add the butter, blending well. Press this mixture into a 9-inch deep-dish pie plate.

To make the filling, beat together the cream cheese and honey in a large bowl. Add the peanut butter and blend well. Fold in the whipped topping and pour the creamy mixture into the prepared crust. Chill and serve garnished with a dollop of hot fudge topping.

Makes 8 to 10 servings

Meringue reaches heights in the South that are impossible to describe. However, to me growing up, meringue was for looks only. I always moved the meringue to the side and got right down to business. *Pie was the hidden treasure under that beautiful, fluffy white.*

Old-Fashioned Vinegar Pie

3   **large eggs**
3   **sticks butter, melted**
3   **tablespoons apple cider vinegar**
1   **cup sugar**
½   **teaspoon almond extract**
1   **(9-inch) unbaked piecrust (page 184)**

Preheat the oven to 400 degrees. Beat the eggs thoroughly in a medium bowl. Add the melted butter, vinegar, sugar, and almond extract and blend well. Pour into the piecrust and bake for 10 minutes. Reduce the oven temperature to 300 degrees and bake for 40 minutes, or until the pie is set in the center and a toothpick inserted in the center comes out clean.

Makes 8 servings

When we talk of missing loved ones who've gone to heaven, inevitably we remember them connected to a recipe. Desserts were usually the sweet connection to our family's angels. If Grandma Walker's applesauce cake with creamy caramel icing, MawMaw Bernice's chocolate pie or coconut pie, and Aunt Carrie's banana pudding come up in our conversations, sooner or later, we've all got out our tissues and we are crying and cooking at the same time.

Desserts in the South are a very emotional thing.

Chocolate-Pecan Chess Pie

In the South, recipes don't just feed our families. They support our schools, our charities, and our causes. This recipe by Pam Holland was one of the major fund-raising tools for her son Adam's school, High Hopes, in Nashville. She baked hundreds of these pies, both full-size and miniature, to support this wonderful haven for children with special needs. Often the pies never made it to the bake sale at the school because the hungry employees at her workplace bought her pies before they got there, but her coworkers' generosity supplied funds to help this beautiful organization thrive.

4	heaping tablespoons unsweetened cocoa powder
1¼	cups sugar
2	large eggs, beaten
¾	cup chopped pecans
4	tablespoons butter, melted
½	cup evaporated milk
1	(9-inch) unbaked piecrust (page 184)

Preheat the oven to 400 degrees. In a medium bowl combine the cocoa, sugar, eggs, pecans, melted butter, and evaporated milk. Pour the pie filling into the unbaked piecrust. Bake for 30 minutes. Allow the pie to cool before serving with ice cream or whipped cream.

Makes 8 servings

Pam's Browned-Butter Icing

Icing can turn a lowly breakfast loaf into a glorious dessert, and this icing from Pam Holland has done that very thing on many occasions at Spotland Productions, which she and her husband, Ben, own and operate. Her homemade goodies are always waiting for clients, friends, and even delivery folks who stop by. This icing is amazing, and in Pam's words, "the easiest thing in the world."

1	**stick unsalted butter**
1	**pound powdered sugar**
1	**tablespoon vanilla extract**
5 to 6	**tablespoons milk**

Melt the butter in a medium saucepan over medium heat. Allow the butter to brown, being very watchful because it can go from nicely browned to burned black in a second. Remove the butter from the heat and beat in the sugar, vanilla, and milk by hand, adjusting the liquid as needed based on the thickness or creaminess desired.

Makes icing for 1 loaf cake or 1 Bundt cake

Peanut Butter Cream Icing

Put icing on a muffin and you've got dessert! This is a yummy way to spread the taste of peanut butter in the most delicious of ways. In addition to muffins, try it on cupcakes, loaf cakes, or Bundt cakes.

1	**tablespoon butter**
1/4	**cup sugar**
2	**tablespoons creamy peanut butter**
1/4	**cup milk**
1 3/4	**cups powdered sugar**
2	**teaspoons vanilla**

Melt the butter over medium-high heat in a saucepan. Add the sugar and peanut butter and stir constantly while cooking for 2 minutes. Gradually add the milk and stir until the mixture is smooth. Remove the mixture from the heat and allow it to cool completely. Gradually stir in the powdered sugar and vanilla and beat just until smooth. Cool before using.

Makes icing for 1 three-layer cake, 2 loaf cakes, 1 Bundt cake, or 24 cupcakes

If you talk to your children, they might listen. If you talk to your children while you bake cookies together, they'll remember what you said and enjoy the talk a whole lot more. Southern moms have known this for years.

Plain White Icing

This is a basic white icing for cupcakes, devil's food cakes, white cakes, or any basic cake. Add sprinkles or fruit for color and variation.

1½	**cups sugar**
½	**cup water**
½	**teaspoon cream of tartar**
⅛	**teaspoon salt**
3	**unbeaten egg whites**
1½	**teaspoons vanilla extract**

Blend the sugar, water, cream of tartar, and salt in a saucepan. Bring to a boil, stirring until the sugar is dissolved. Remove the icing from the heat and while still hot, slowly blend in the unbeaten egg whites with a handheld electric mixer until stiff peaks form. Beat in the vanilla.

Makes icing for 1 three-layer cake or 1 (11 x 9-inch) sheet cake

Cream Cheese Icing

This is a great icing for banana nut cake, a variation on red velvet cake (page 178), or any spice cake.

1³/₄   **cups powdered sugar**
¹/₂   **cup cream cheese, chilled**
1   **teaspoon vanilla extract**

In a medium bowl beat all the ingredients with a handheld electric mixer until just blended. Topping this icing with 2 tablespoons finely chopped pecans or walnuts and/or ¹/₄ cup grated coconut makes for a nice variation.

Makes icing for 1 loaf cake, 1 (11 x 9-inch) sheet cake, or 12 cupcakes

Mayhaw Jelly

Mayhaws are wild coral-colored berries, similar to wild cranberries, that grow abundantly in the South. We pick them to make this beautiful jelly with a light, sweet, luscious flavor that makes homemade biscuits better than you could think possible. This fruit has become so popular that it is now sold at fresh fruit markets, roadside stands, and you-pick-it orchards all over the Southeast.

1   gallon mayhaw berries
1   (1.75-ounce) package fruit pectin
5½   cups sugar

To make mayhaw juice, bring the berries to a boil in a large stockpot with just enough water to cover them, and simmer until the berries are completely tender and foam appears on top of them. Push the berries down to push out the juice. When the foam appears, skim it off and discard it, and strain out any berries or residue by pouring the juice through cheesecloth. Do this twice. The first boiling will be a stronger, more robust juice. Repeat the process with the same berries to get the second, milder juice. Skim the foam each time and discard before you strain through the cheesecloth. Blend the juice from these two "boilings" together. Add 5 cups of the juice to a stockpot or large pot (refrigerate any extra juice for other recipes). Mix in the fruit pectin and bring to a rolling boil that cannot be stirred down. Then add the sugar and bring to a boil again that cannot be stirred down. Boil for 1 minute. Remove the jelly from the heat and set aside, skimming off any foam and discarding. Fill 6 hot sterile half-pint jars to within ½ inch from the tops, clean any residue from the jar tops, and seal with boiled lids.

Makes 6 half-pints

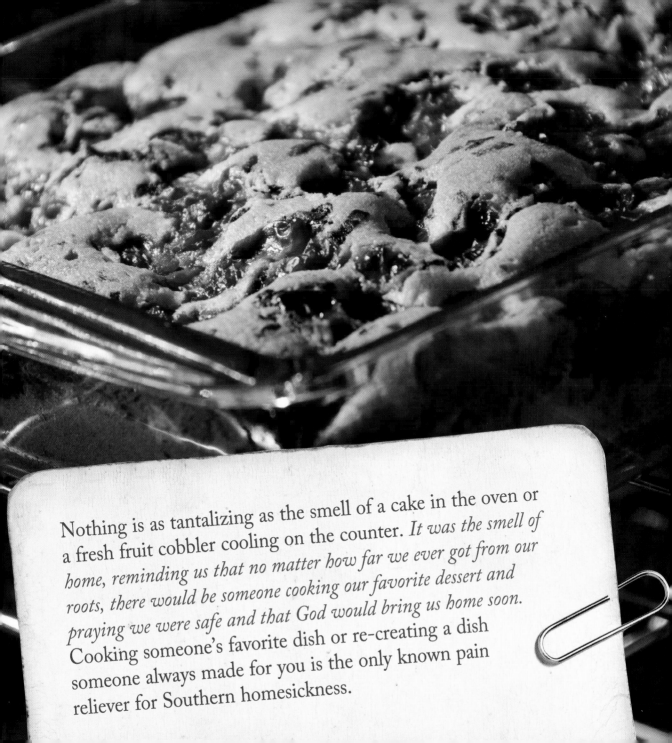

Nothing is as tantalizing as the smell of a cake in the oven or a fresh fruit cobbler cooling on the counter. *It was the smell of home, reminding us that no matter how far we ever got from our roots, there would be someone cooking our favorite dessert and praying we were safe and that God would bring us home soon.* Cooking someone's favorite dish or re-creating a dish someone always made for you is the only known pain reliever for Southern homesickness.

Barbecue Joints, Catfish Kitchens, and Meat and Threes
Eating Out Southern-Style

I can remember my first foray into an expensive New York restaurant shortly after moving from the South. I was served two bite-size pieces of decorative meat, swathed in sauce that reached to the edge of the plate with a colorful drizzle to make the plate appear full. There was a carrot frilled to resemble a garnish. I was thrilled with the beautiful presentation and absolutely horrified when I realized this was not a sample of the food but the actual entrée, for the same price I would pay for a nice pedicure. In the South, a restaurant experience means the food is piled high and you get three sides, a salad, pie, and sweet tea. All that, and the biscuits are free. Yes, I like dining out where you don't have to eat when you get home because you're starving. I love re-creating my favorite restaurant experiences at home too. The food in this chapter is pure comfort!

Sweet Georgia Brown Fruit Tea

I named my fruit-tea concoction after Georgia peaches and a song that I love.

2	cups water
2	quart-size tea bags
½	cup sugar
1	cup orange juice concentrate
1	cup lemonade concentrate
1	cup pineapple juice
½	cup peach nectar
2	cups cold water
	Thinly sliced citrus for garnish

Bring the 2 cups water to a boil in a pot, add the tea bags, turn off the heat, and allow the tea to steep for 15 minutes. Remove the tea bags, add the sugar to the warm tea, and stir until the sugar is well dissolved. Pour the tea into a 2-quart pitcher and while warm add the orange juice concentrate, lemonade concentrate, pineapple juice, and peach nectar. Stir until the juices are dissolved. Add the 2 cups cold water, filling to within 1 inch of the top of the pitcher. Serve this sweet drink over ice with citrus garnishes. For the after-five crowd, this can easily become a tall, refreshing cocktail laced with bourbon, rum, or amaretto.

Makes 2 quarts

Hushpuppies

3	cups vegetable oil for deep-frying
1	cup cornmeal
½	teaspoon salt
2	teaspoons baking powder
1	large egg
1	small onion, chopped
¼ to ½	cup milk

In a deep fryer or large cast-iron skillet, heat the oil to 375 degrees. Meanwhile, in a medium bowl combine the cornmeal, salt, baking powder, egg, onion, and milk and mix well. Drop by tablespoonfuls into the hot oil. Fry until a deep golden brown on both sides. The hushpuppies should float in the oil. Remove when done and drain on paper towels. Serve while hot.

Makes 6 to 8 hushpuppies

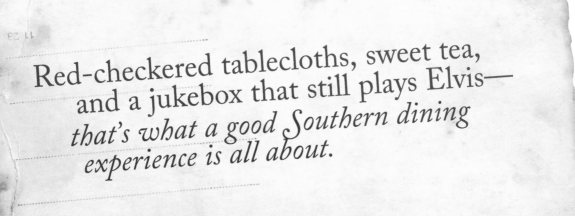

Red-checkered tablecloths, sweet tea, and a jukebox that still plays Elvis— that's what a good Southern dining experience is all about.

Hot-Water Bread

One of my favorite cornbread recipes is hot-water bread, in which the milk is replaced with boiling water. When the batter is fried, the water cooks out and the result is a deliciously crisp corn fritter that is delightful served with fish or vegetables, or dipped in brown gravy.

2	**cups water**
	Enough vegetable oil to fill skillet with ½ inch oil
3/4	**cup cornmeal**
½	**cup all-purpose flour**
¼	**cup finely chopped onion (optional)**
1	**teaspoon salt**
1	**teaspoon sugar**
1	**large egg**

Boil the water in a kettle while heating the oil in a large skillet. In a large bowl combine the cornmeal, flour, onion if using, salt, sugar, and egg, beating well. Pour in the boiling water. This mixture should be easy to pour. If it seems too thick, just add more water. Carefully put tablespoonfuls of batter into the hot oil and cook on both sides until medium to dark golden brown, about 2 minutes on each side.

Makes 6 to 8 crunchy flatbread cakes

The best Southern food is messy, so don't worry about spilling any. We are used to that here in the South. Pickles and raw onion come with your food. If you are having catfish, you usually get your white beans and French fries served as sides, only we call 'em "fixin's." The waiters always say, *"Save room for dessert,"* which, of course, we never do. So if you really want to have dessert, you'd better eat it first. That's the *only* way to save room for dessert in the South.

Creamy, Dreamy Coleslaw Dressing

½	**cup white vinegar**
½	**cup sugar**
½	**cup cream**
3	**egg yolks**
2	**tablespoons poppy seeds**
½	**teaspoon white pepper**

In a medium saucepan bring the vinegar and sugar to a boil. In a small bowl mix the cream and egg yolks, beating well. Stir the cream mixture into the vinegar mixture. Cook until thickened but do not boil. Stir in the poppy seeds and pepper. Pour the dressing over chopped cabbage for coleslaw or on the vegetables of your choice.

Makes 1½ cups

Kickin' Tartar Sauce

If you are frying your own catfish, why not whip up your own tartar sauce?

1	cup chopped dill pickles or dill pickle relish
³/₄	cup minced onion
¹/₂	teaspoon minced garlic
2	cups mayonnaise
1	tablespoon lemon juice
¹/₂	teaspoon salt
¹/₈	teaspoon white pepper
¹/₈	teaspoon cayenne pepper

Combine all the ingredients in a small bowl. Cover and refrigerate overnight so all the flavors are absorbed.

Makes 2 pints

Some of the best food I've ever had was in buildings that look like the most run-down shacks you've ever seen. Don't ever judge food in the South by the quality of the table linens or by the peeling paint on the sign out front.

Black-Eyed Pea Soup

One of my favorite restaurants growing up was the Plantation Manor in Alexandria, Louisiana. It was the only place I had ever been in my young life that served meals in courses. The soup course was served in a tiny cup with deep-fried corn "fingers" for dipping. The soups were unusually Southern and uncommonly delicious. From squash bisque to split pea soup to black-eyed pea soup, it was the best part of the meal!

1	pound ground pork sausage
1	small onion, minced
1	green bell pepper, chopped
½	teaspoon minced garlic
4	cups cooked black-eyed peas
1	(10-ounce) can diced tomatoes with green chiles
2	cups chicken broth
½	teaspoon salt
½	teaspoon pepper
	Tabasco sauce for serving

Cook the pork sausage in a deep skillet with the onion, bell pepper, and garlic until the sausage is browned, the onion is clear, and the pepper is tender. Pour off the excess grease through a colander. Pour the meat mixture into a stockpot. Stir in the peas, tomatoes, broth, salt, and pepper. Cover and simmer the soup on medium for 20 to 25 minutes, stirring often, letting the peas become more and more creamy. Serve hot with Tabasco sauce as a condiment. Hot corn fritters are great for dipping in this soup.

Makes 6 to 8 servings

Stewed Irish Potato Soup

My Aunt Lessie Butler kept me when I was six years old and had the chicken pox. I was miserable with itching, but she made me stewed "Arsh" taters and cornbread and taught me to play Scrabble. It was the best meal I'd ever had, I thought. She just laughed and told me it was just stewed taters and cornbread. I think she knew that good comfort food and the time spent playing Scrabble with her and Uncle Carl was just the thing I needed to make me forget my polka-dotted self. It worked!

6	cups new potatoes
1	stalk celery, chopped
1	medium onion, chopped
1	(12-ounce) can evaporated milk
3	tablespoons butter
1	teaspoon salt
1	teaspoon pepper
2	tablespoons all-purpose flour
8	ounces heavy cream
6	slices bacon, fried and crumbled

To peel new potatoes easily, partially boil (parboil) them, allow them to cool, and pop the skins off. Simmer the skinned potatoes, celery, and onion in enough water to just cover them in a large soup pot. When the potatoes are tender, add the evaporated milk, butter, salt, and pepper. Create a slurry by blending the flour with ¼ cup water in a small bowl. Stir until all the lumps are gone and add to the potatoes. Stir and simmer the potatoes until a thick gravy begins to form. Pour in the cream and allow the soup to warm completely before serving. Top the soup with crumbled bacon. This is a great comfort soup served with cornbread or hot-water bread (page 214).

Makes 6 to 8 servings

Don't miss the daily special at a meat and three. It's not what they are trying to get rid of like in some places. Usually a daily special is what the cook and the proprietor were in the mood for that day. It's always good, and always worth trying.

Creamy Mashed Potatoes

6 to 8	medium red potatoes
2	teaspoons salt
1	teaspoon pepper
4	tablespoons butter
½	cup milk
1	tablespoon sour cream
½	cup heavy cream

Wash the potatoes and boil in a large saucepan of salted water until tender, so the skins can be removed easily. Remove the skins. Mash the potatoes with a potato masher, and using a handheld electric mixer on low, gradually mix in the salt, pepper, butter, milk, sour cream, and heavy cream until all are integrated. Increase the speed of the mixer little by little until finally whipping the potatoes until they are creamy. Serve hot with gravy, or dotted with butter in the serving dish.

Makes 4 to 6 servings

Fresh Okra and Tomatoes

1	slice bacon
1	medium onion, chopped
4 to 5	tomatoes, peeled and chopped
4	cups sliced okra (about ½-inch slices)
1	teaspoon salt
1	jalapeño pepper, seeded and sliced (optional)

Fry the bacon in the bottom of a 3-quart pot and crumble it. Sauté the onion in the bacon grease until the onion is clear. Stir in the tomatoes and continue to cook them until they are hot and bubbly. At that time, fold in the okra, salt, and jalapeño pepper if using. Cover, reduce the heat, and simmer for 20 to 30 minutes, until the okra is tender but not falling apart. Overcooking can make the okra become "ropey" or slimy.

Makes 6 servings

Buttered Baby Carrots

On almost every meat and three menu, buttered carrots appear. They are simple and good for you, and add color to your plate, which is so important at the Southern table.

4	**cups baby carrots**
1	**teaspoon salt**
1/2	**teaspoon sugar**
2	**tablespoons butter**
3 1/2	**cups water**

Add all the ingredients to a saucepan and bring to a boil. Cover, reduce the heat, and simmer until the carrots are tender, 20 to 25 minutes.

Makes 4 servings

Green Beans and Ham

½   cup chopped ham (country ham or cured ham)
1   tablespoon vegetable oil
1½   cups water
1   teaspoon sugar
1   teaspoon salt
2   pounds fresh green beans, snapped

Brown the ham in the oil in a 3-quart pot. When it's browned, add the water, sugar, and salt and bring everything to a boil. Add the beans and stir to integrate the flavors. Cover the pot, reduce the heat, and simmer for 25 to 30 minutes, or until the beans are tender.

Makes 6 servings

Vinegar or pickled pepper sauce is on all the tables in the South. It's poured on vegetables and fried catfish. It gives it that sour kick we like. You will get a dish of cut lemons too. You can squeeze them over the fish, squeeze them in your iced tea, and use them to wash the grease off your fingers when you are through.
Didn't I tell you that in Southern joints, you can always use your fingers?

Skillet-Fried Potatoes

Home fries, fried taters, French-fried tater rounds—whatever you call them, they are potatoes peeled, sliced, and cooked hot with onions until they are crunchy on the outside. Then they are covered, placed over reduced heat, and allowed to cook until tender. Though my friend Kim McLean taught me how to do this, her father, Bob McLean, gets the credit. This is his signature dish, and I have yet to do them as well. But I've been assured practice makes perfect.

½	cup vegetable oil
4	cups sliced potatoes
1	medium onion, sliced
1½	teaspoons salt (Bob swears by his hickory-flavored seasoning salt)
½	teaspoon pepper
1½	tablespoons bacon bits (optional)

In a large deep skillet heat the oil on medium-high heat. Add the potatoes and onion and sear them on the outside for crunch. Turn the potatoes from the bottom up as they brown on the outside, gradually sprinkling the salt and pepper on the layers. After 15 minutes, or when the potatoes have a golden edge to them, cover, reduce the heat, and allow them to cook until tender, 20 to 25 minutes more. Serve while hot, garnished with bacon bits if desired.

Makes 4 to 6 servings

Some of the best eateries in the South are hot, cooled with ceiling fans and a screen door at the entrance. You don't have to dress up to go, and no one cares if you tuck your napkin in your collar.

Always save room for dessert, or take some home.

You don't want to miss a thing when it comes to these humble eating establishments.

Two-Pot Chicken and Sausage Gumbo

Gumbo filé is a ground spice used often in my home state. It is added to gumbos after they are served, never while cooking. The tender shoots of the sassafras bush are harvested after the plant has bloomed and leafed out, and are only to be gathered in the dark of night. The shoots are dried and ground for use in gumbos. We've always found it much easier to just buy a jar of the stuff at the grocery store, and sleep on really dark nights.

1   cup vegetable oil, divided
1   cup all-purpose flour
2   pounds boneless, skinless chicken breasts, cut in chunks

2	pounds kielbasa sausage, sliced in rounds
1	cup chopped onions
1	cup chopped celery
1	cup chopped bell peppers
½	teaspoon minced garlic
2	teaspoons salt
½	teaspoon pepper
½	teaspoon Cajun seasoning
6	cups water or chicken broth
2	cups sliced fresh okra (about ½-inch slices) (optional)
½	cup canned diced tomatoes with green chiles, drained (optional)
	Gumbo filé powder for serving (optional)

In a Dutch oven make a roux by heating ¾ cup of the oil and adding the flour, stirring constantly until a dark brown color. Do *not* leave this unattended or unstirred. It will burn easily. (Jarred roux or roux mixes can be used as well.) When the roux is dark but not burned, remove the Dutch oven from the heat. Heat the remaining ¼ cup oil in another large pot and sauté the chicken, sausage, and onions until almost done. Put the meat mixture in the Dutch oven with the roux. Stir in the celery, bell peppers, garlic, salt, pepper, and Cajun seasoning. Add enough water or chicken broth to cover the entire gumbo by at least 1 inch, stirring to fully integrate the roux with the mixture. Bring the contents to a boil, stirring to blend well. Cover, reduce the heat, and simmer for about 45 minutes. If you are using okra, flash cook the okra while the gumbo is boiling. Spread the okra on a baking sheet and bake in the oven at 400 degrees for 20 to 30 minutes, or until slightly crunchy on the outside. This prevents the okra from getting "ropey" or slimy. Add the okra and optional tomatoes to the gumbo after it has cooked for 45 minutes and stir to blend well. Cover and cook for 15 minutes longer. If at any time the gumbo seems too thick, add more water or chicken broth. Serve over cooked rice, and sprinkle with gumbo filé in individual bowls, if desired.

Makes 8 to 10 servings

Creamy Jambalaya Pasta

I am always throwing things in a pot with cooked pasta. I made traditional jambalaya when I was a guest on the Vicki Lawrence Show *years ago. This is one of my experiments on that theme that turned out quite well. Of course, with these ingredients and a little cream sauce, how could one go wrong?*

7	cups chicken broth, divided
1	(16-ounce) package rotini pasta
¼	teaspoon salt
¼	teaspoon pepper
3	tablespoons olive oil
2	cups chunked chicken breast (bite-size chunks)
2	cups sliced link sausage (smoked, kielbasa, or andouille)
2	teaspoons minced garlic
1	medium onion, chopped
1	large green bell pepper, chopped
½	cup finely chopped celery
2	teaspoons liquid smoke
4	tablespoons Worcestershire sauce
2	tablespoons Cajun seasoning
2	(10-ounce) cans diced tomatoes with green chiles, drained
2	cups uncooked shrimp, washed, peeled, and deveined with tails removed
1½	cups heavy cream

In a large pot bring the chicken broth to a boil. Add the pasta, salt, and pepper and cook the pasta in the broth as if it were water. Cook for 7 to 10 minutes on a high boil, until the pasta is just tender. Drain, reserving the broth for later in the recipe. In a large skillet heat the oil and sauté the chicken, sausage, garlic, onion, green pepper, and celery for 10 to 15 minutes. Add the liquid smoke, Worcestershire sauce, and Cajun seasoning as the mixture cooks, stirring periodically to ensure even cooking. When the chicken is done, the onion is clear, and the vegetables are tender, combine all the ingredients, including the pasta, in the original large pot and place over medium heat. Add the tomatoes, blending well. When the tomatoes are hot, add 1 cup of the reserved chicken broth and the shrimp, blending. Cover and allow to simmer for 5 minutes. In the last 3 minutes of cooking, stir in the cream. Serve immediately, while everything is warm. Reserve any leftover chicken broth for another recipe.

Makes 6 to 8 servings

It always tickles me to see the signs for Southern food joints.

Now, a restaurant might have a lovely sign, lit with spotlights, with a Southern plantation flair. A "joint" will have anything to get your attention, from flashing lights, to neon, to a larger-than-life smiling catfish dressed in a straw hat, wielding a cane pole. Barbecue joints almost always have a dancing, smiling pig inviting you to partake. Although most pigs aren't dancing their way into the smoker, just look for the smiling piggies to guide you to a great meal if you are in the South.

When you are in the South, don't be surprised if you get called honey, darlin', sugar, or baby by someone taking your order.

You could take offense, but why not just take it as a compliment?

Whiskey-Butternut Glaze

Use this glaze on the grill with salmon or chicken, or drizzle it on baked sweet potatoes. To make a luscious sauce for bread pudding, stir ½ cup cream into the cooked glaze after it has been removed from the heat.

2	**sticks butter**
½	**cup firmly packed dark brown sugar**
½	**cup bourbon**
¼	**teaspoon salt**
2	**tablespoons honey**
¼	**cup finely chopped pecans**

In a saucepan over medium heat, melt the butter and stir in the sugar, bourbon, salt, honey, and pecans until all granules of sugar are dissolved. Remove from the heat.

Makes 2 cups

Bar-B-Kick Sauce

This spicy sauce is incredible on chicken, brushed on in the last 10 minutes of grilling. It adds snap to hot wings or salmon, and brings new life to ordinary pork ribs.

1	teaspoon cayenne pepper
1	teaspoon freshly ground black pepper
1	(6-ounce) can tomato paste
	Juice of 1 lemon
1/2	teaspoon Worcestershire sauce
2	cups apple cider vinegar
1/2	cup firmly packed brown sugar
2	tablespoons salt
2	tablespoons chili powder
2	tablespoons ketchup

Combine all the ingredients in a saucepan and bring to a boil. Boil for 5 minutes, reduce the heat, and stir until the sauce thickens. Refrigerate overnight so the flavors in the sauce can mingle.

Makes about 3 cups

Lemon Butter-B-Q Sauce

This is wonderful on chicken or fish cooked on the grill, or broiled in the oven.

2	**sticks butter**
	Juice from 6 lemons
1	**teaspoon pepper**
1	**teaspoon Tabasco sauce**
1	**tablespoon salt**
1	**tablespoon garlic powder**
1	**tablespoon celery salt**
2	**tablespoons Worcestershire sauce**
1	**tablespoon honey**

Melt the butter in a saucepan on low heat and, one by one, blend in the lemon juice, pepper, Tabasco sauce, salt, garlic powder, celery salt, Worcestershire sauce, and honey until mixed well.

Makes 1½ cups

Sweet Grillin' Sauce

Marinate meats or chicken in this sauce overnight before grilling.

1	**(8-ounce) can tomato sauce**
¼	**cup lemon juice**
3	**tablespoons brown sugar**
2	**tablespoons white vinegar**
1	**teaspoon Worcestershire sauce**
1	**teaspoon liquid smoke**
1	**teaspoon prepared mustard**
2	**tablespoons maple syrup**
⅛	**teaspoon pepper**
⅛	**teaspoon cayenne pepper**
⅛	**teaspoon garlic powder**

In a saucepan bring all the ingredients to a boil, stirring constantly. Reduce the heat and simmer slowly for 15 to 20 minutes.

Makes 1½ cups

You can buy barbecued pork by the pound in the South, at almost any joint on any roadside. It's good, smoked out back, and melts in your mouth. For a fourth of the pound price, you can get almost the same amount of meat (a pound) by ordering a sandwich. *If you know how to order in the South, you can really get a good value.*

Barbecue Dry Rub

Rub this mixture into meats before smoking or before cooking in a pit barbecue.

1	**pound brown sugar**
1	**cup salt**
1½	**ounces paprika**
1	**tablespoon black pepper**
1½	**teaspoons red pepper**
1	**teaspoon cinnamon**
2	**tablespoons garlic powder**
2	**tablespoons dry mustard**

Sift all the ingredients together at least three times to make sure everything blends completely.
Store in a closed jar or dry canister.

Makes 2½ cups

Pork Chops in a Pot

Dredging a seasoned pork chop in flour and deep-frying it is the default Southern delivery method, but this recipe is delicious and you can put it in the oven, prepare the rest of the meal, and still have time to read the latest issue of Southern Living.

¾	**cup vegetable oil**
8	**pork chops**
1	**tablespoon salt**
1	**tablespoon pepper**
1	**medium yellow onion, chopped**
1½	**cups water**

In a Dutch oven heat the oil. Sprinkle the pork chops with salt and pepper on both sides. When the oil is hot, sear each pork chop on both sides, browning completely but not cooking through. When each chop is browned, set aside on a platter until the rest of the chops are browned. When the chops are browned, carefully pour out the excess oil into a pan to discard, leaving a very small amount in the bottom of the Dutch oven. Add the onion and cook on medium heat until it is clear, stirring constantly and scraping the sides of the pot to avoid any burning. Preheat the oven to 350 degrees. When the onion is done, add the water to the pot. Layer the pork chops in the pot and bring the water to a boil. Cover the pot and bake for 1 hour, until the chops are tender.

Makes 8 servings

"All you can eat" is a tough thing in the South. Everything tastes so good, you will leave with a stomachache if you follow that principle. Some places have opted for the phrase "All you care to eat." I think they should have a big sign over the buffet that just says "More than anyone could possibly eat" and leave it at that.

The Easiest Meatloaf in the World

Ain't nobody don't like a good meatloaf! And this one is foolproof. Leftovers make the best meatloaf sandwiches in the world. My friend Kim McLean shared this recipe with me, and it's one that even the most finicky eater will find comfort in.

1½	pounds ground chuck (this also works well with ground turkey)
2	large eggs, beaten
1	cup uncooked oats
1	(8-ounce) can tomato sauce
1	medium onion, chopped
1	medium green bell pepper, chopped
1½	teaspoons salt
1	teaspoon pepper
1	cup ketchup

Preheat the oven to 350 degrees. Blend the meat, eggs, oats, tomato sauce, onion, bell pepper, salt, and pepper with your hands in a large bowl. Pack the meatloaf firmly in an 8½ x 4½-inch loaf pan and bake for 1 hour and 15 minutes. Remove from the oven and cover the top of the meatloaf with a layer of ketchup. Return the loaf to the oven and bake for 5 minutes to heat the ketchup. Remove the loaf from the oven and allow it to cool for 5 minutes before serving.

Makes 8 servings

Louisiana Hot Salmon Croquettes

These are a spicy version of an old Southern favorite. They are savory enough to eat alone, but can also be served with ranch dressing, tartar sauce, or ketchup. Wilted lettuce, buttered carrots, and bayou kidney beans are wonderful side items.

1	(15.5-ounce) can salmon (skinless, boneless), drained
2	large eggs
2	tablespoons all-purpose flour
1	teaspoon Cajun seasoning
½	medium onion, chopped fine
½	teaspoon minced garlic
¼	teaspoon Louisiana hot sauce
½	teaspoon Worcestershire sauce
¼	cup shredded Asiago cheese
½	cup vegetable oil
1	cup cornmeal

Combine the salmon, eggs, flour, Cajun seasoning, onion, garlic, hot sauce, Worcestershire sauce, and cheese. Heat the oil in a large skillet. Roll the salmon mixture into balls about 2 inches in diameter, and coat the balls with the cornmeal. Put the salmon balls in the hot oil and press into patties, frying until golden brown on both sides, about 2 minutes on each side. Remove, drain on paper towels, and serve immediately.

Makes 6 servings

> In the South, if you pay for a meal and you don't leave stuffed, you feel shortchanged.

Salmon 'n' Grits

4	salmon fillets	1/2	teaspoon pepper
1/2	cup liquid smoke	4	tablespoons butter
1/2	cup Italian salad dressing	2	slices American cheese
1	cup quick-cooking grits	1/4	cup grated sharp Cheddar cheese
3 1/2	cups water	4	slices turkey bacon
1/2	teaspoon salt	1/4	cup shredded Parmesan cheese

Marinate the salmon fillets in the liquid smoke and the Italian salad dressing. Cover and refrigerate overnight.

In a saucepan cook the grits in the water according to the package directions, adding the salt and pepper as the grits begin to cook. Heat a large griddle or skillet and melt the butter over medium heat. Add the American and Cheddar cheeses to the grits. Stir and allow the cheeses to melt. Remove the grits from the heat, or reduce the heat to low to keep warm. When the skillet is heated, place the fillets in the skillet, increase the temperature to high, cook for 2 to 3 minutes, flip the fillets, and cook for 2 to 3 minutes on the other side. Use the marinade to coat the salmon as it cooks. While the salmon cooks, microwave the turkey bacon, covered in a paper towel or between two paper plates, for 4 to 5 minutes, checking after 4 minutes. Dish equal amounts of cheese grits onto 4 plates, creating a bed for the salmon. Remove the salmon when it flakes, after about 6 minutes of cooking time, and place one fillet on each bed of grits. Crumble one slice of turkey bacon on each salmon fillet and top with the Parmesan cheese.

Makes 4 servings

Tuna Boats

If a hushpuppy and tuna salad had a baby, tuna boats would be it. Created from a lowly can of tuna, this fun little croquette is perfect for any time you are in the mood for a fish fry, but haven't had time to put a hook in the water.

1	**(6-ounce) can tuna**
1	**medium onion, chopped fine**
2	**heaping tablespoons all-purpose flour**
1	**heaping teaspoon baking powder**
1	**teaspoon salt**
1/2	**teaspoon pepper**
1	**large egg**
2	**cups vegetable oil for frying**

Blend the tuna, onion, flour, baking powder, salt, pepper, and egg in a bowl. Heat the oil in a skillet. Make heaping-tablespoon-size croquettes from the tuna mixture and carefully spoon each into the hot oil. (Don't drop them in the oil; just ease them off the spoon.) Fry until the tuna boats are golden on both sides, about 3 minutes on each side, and they float (hence the name). Remove, drain on paper towels, and serve hot.

Makes 6 to 8 croquettes

If you go to the same restaurant twice in the South and get the same waitress, don't be surprised if she remembers your name, what you like to drink, and anything particular you prefer about your meal.

Impress-the-Yankees Fried Chicken Tenders

During my two years in New York City, where I modeled for Ford and studied writing at NYU, I gave up on satisfying my homesick need for fried chicken anywhere but my kitchen. This little recipe drew all my neighbors to my apartment eventually. Do not make these fluffy, spicy tenders if you aren't in the mood for company.

12	chicken tenders	2	large eggs
3	cups buttermilk, divided	¼	teaspoon Tabasco sauce
2	teaspoons salt, divided	2	cups vegetable oil for deep-frying
1	teaspoon pepper, divided	2	cups all-purpose flour
3	teaspoons Cajun seasoning, divided		

Soak the chicken tenders, covered, in the refrigerator in 2 cups of the buttermilk overnight or for at least 8 hours.

The next day remove the tenders from the milk and put them in a large bowl. Discard the milk. In a small bowl combine 1 teaspoon of the salt, ½ teaspoon of the pepper, and 1½ teaspoons of the Cajun seasoning. Cover the chicken tenders thoroughly with the spice mixture. In a separate small bowl beat the eggs well and then add the remaining 1 cup buttermilk and the Tabasco sauce, continuing to beat well. In a large cast-iron skillet, heat the oil to 375 degrees. Test the temperature of the oil with flour. It should bubble when ready. Combine the flour with the remaining 1 teaspoon salt, ½ teaspoon pepper, and 1½ teaspoons Cajun seasoning. Coat the individual tenders with the egg mixture and then coat with the seasoned flour. Carefully place in the hot oil. Fry several tenders at a time until golden brown, 6 to 8 minutes, turning often. Transfer to a platter lined with paper towels and serve hot.

Makes 6 servings

If you are going to eat out, you tell people what meat you are going to eat. If you are going to eat chicken, it's fried chicken. If you are going to eat fish, it's catfish and it's fried. If you are going for barbecue, it's just understood you are going to get pork, even though Texas features beef barbecue. Of course, Texas is its own country, and not officially Southern, either. Texans are proud of that fact, and have a right to be. *So let's get this straight: Chicken and catfish are fried. Pork is barbecued unless it's chops, and then it's fried or smothered. Beef is roast.* There aren't many people in the South saying they're going out to eat "vegetarian salad bar with tofu cubes," but we'll be real polite when you ask if that's available. Please be polite when we say no.

Fried Catfish

Fillets are easy to eat because you never have to worry about bones, but our family liked whole catfish. It's a personal preference, but if you don't mind cooking a little longer, and filleting the fish on your own plate after cooking, then a whole catfish offers more flavor, tenderness, and flaky white meat than a fillet. Cajun seasoning, such as Tony Chachere's, Zatarain's, or Uncle Leon's, can replace salt and pepper in this recipe if you like a spicy kick.

8   **(8-ounce) catfish fillets**
       Salt to taste
       Pepper to taste
2   **cups cornmeal**
2   **cups vegetable oil for frying**

Season the catfish fillets with salt and pepper on each side. Dredge in the cornmeal. Heat the oil in a cast-iron skillet or Dutch oven on high. Test the oil's heat with a pinch of cornmeal. Once the cornmeal sizzles, gently place the fish in the skillet, cover, and cook about 2 minutes per side, or until the fish is a light golden color. Remove, drain on paper towels, and serve hot.

Makes 8 servings

Good Ol' Nanner Puddin'

It's a Southern thing to shorten words to a delightful original speak that makes everything sound more endearing. We drop the g's, we drawl the syllables, and we love things the way our granny said them. "Nanner puddin'" is one of those common delicacies that just sounds more authentically Southern than "banana pudding" ever could, even though it's the same thing.

⅓	cup cornstarch
½	teaspoon salt
1	cup sugar
4	cups evaporated milk, divided
4	tablespoons butter
2	teaspoons vanilla extract
36	vanilla wafers
5	bananas, sliced
1	(16-ounce) container frozen whipped topping, thawed

In a small bowl combine the cornstarch, salt, sugar, and 1 cup of the milk. Bring the remaining 3 cups milk to a boil in a large saucepan and add the sugar mixture. Stir constantly over medium heat as the custard thickens. Reduce the heat and add the butter and vanilla. When the pudding is thick, remove it from the heat and allow it to cool. In a large dessert bowl or clear compote bowl, layer the vanilla wafers, bananas, and pudding, repeating the layers in that order until all the pudding is used. Top with the whipped topping, cover, and chill the pudding before serving. An interesting twist is to use chocolate chip cookies instead of vanilla wafers for "chocolate chip" banana pudding.

Makes 6 to 8 servings

A meat and three guarantees you get meat (pork, beef, fish, or chicken) in huge amounts, including the gravy. The sides will be any vegetable you can imagine, simmering in bacon and butter. The desserts will have icing, meringue, or if you are trying to diet, some sort of Jell-O. Everything will be fresh. Everything will be good. Nothing will be low-fat. *Just enjoy the meal, and take a thirty-minute walk afterward.* The best thing about a meat and three is you get enough food for two, and it's always less than ten bucks.

Piña Colada Poke Cake

This is an adaptation of my friend Ruth Passons' moist, rich coconut poke cake. She's from East Tennessee and one of the most gifted cooks and loving people I've ever known. When you've visited Ruth, you've been fed and loved on and you're ready to face another day.

1   (18.25-ounce) package French vanilla cake mix
½   cup crushed pineapple, drained
½   teaspoon coconut extract
1   (14-ounce) can cream of coconut
1   (14-ounce) can sweetened condensed milk
1   (16-ounce) container frozen whipped topping, thawed (French vanilla flavored if you can find it)
1   (8-ounce) package flaked coconut
1   cup maraschino cherries, drained

Prepare the cake mix batter according to the package instructions and pour into a 13 x 9-inch pan. Blend the pineapple and coconut extract with the batter and bake according to the package directions. Meanwhile, blend together the cream of coconut and the sweetened condensed milk in a medium bowl. When the cake is done, remove it from the oven and poke holes all over the top of the cake with a toothpick. Spread the cream mixture over the hot cake while it is still in the pan so the sweet, creamy liquid will melt down into the cake. Let the cake cool completely in the pan. In a medium bowl mix the whipped topping with the flaked coconut. Spread the topping on top of the cake. Place the cherries in rows across the top of the cake so that each piece gets at least one "cherry on top." Keep this cake covered in the refrigerator.

Makes 8 servings

You can tell where people are from in the South by the way they want their barbecue sauce. Thick and spicy sweet is Deep South; add a little fire when you're dipping into the edge of East Texas. Head toward the Carolinas, and tart, thin vinegar sauce wins out. Along the Mississippi Delta, the dry rubs and pulled pork with no sauce at all, with meat that falls off the bone, will tickle your fancy. From the pig in the ground, to beef briskets on the grill, to Boston butts in elaborate black barbecue pits that require an eighteen-wheeler to move them, *barbecue is not just food in the South—it's a lifestyle.*

Afterword

It is my hope that readers not only experience these recipes,
but also create meals with their families, talk for hours around the dinner table, and
come to understand that love is the most important ingredient of any recipe.

Acknowledgments

My mother, Patricia Walker Ford, taught me to cook. More accurately, she forced me to cook and to take home economics (thanks, Mom). She is a gifted artist and writer who encouraged constant creativity in the kitchen. Cooking was just another piece of art that she created for our taste buds to appreciate. She has always been courageous in trying new things, growing new things, and expanding our horizons. She has spent most of her life as an elementary school teacher; as a mother to my sister, Faith, and me; and as a devoted wife. In her heart she has always seen the art in everything and, in so doing, she has taught me to do the same. She was with me from page one to the final period of this book. Thank you, Mom, for always making me think the biggest dreams were achievable. It is because of you that Faith and I believe that anything is possible.

My thanks also to my best friend, Kim McLean, who helped me by testing, typing, and transcribing recipes throughout this entire process; my late grandmothers, Cora Roberts Walker and Bernice Eubanks Ford, who always made food their gift of love to us; my sister, Faith Ford, the gourmet of the family and the most loving hostess I have ever known; Brenda Allen and the ladies of my beautiful Little White Church on the Hill in Kingston Springs, Tennessee; Mrs. Girlinghouse and Mrs. Watkins, my home economics teachers in Pineville, Louisiana; and my family of great cooks who have created a legacy of home-cooked meals throughout my life, Joe Johnston, Brenda Walker Johnston, Sue Cooper Walker, Ruth Passons, Marilyn Allen, Pam Holland, Pepper Saucier, and all those people whose handwritten recipes were found in family Bibles and old cookbooks.

Index